Alkalise Me

How I Reversed Diabetes in Five Weeks

Sharon D. Jones

AuthorHouse™ UK Ltd.
500 Avebury Boulevard
Central Milton Keynes, MK9 2BE
www.authorhouse.co.uk
Phone: 08001974150

©2011 Sharon D. Jones. All rights reserved.

No part of this book may be reproduced, stored in a retrieval system, or transmitted by any means without the written permission of the author.

First published by AuthorHouse 5/04/2011

ISBN: 978-1-4567-7715-9 (sc)
ISBN: 978-1-4567-8147-7 (ebk)

Any people depicted in stock imagery provided by Thinkstock are models, and such images are being used for illustrative purposes only. Certain stock imagery © Thinkstock.

This book is printed on acid-free paper.

Because of the dynamic nature of the Internet, any web addresses or links contained in this book may have changed since publication and may no longer be valid. The views expressed in this work are solely those of the author and do not necessarily reflect the views of the publisher, and the publisher hereby disclaims any responsibility for them.

May 2006.
After spending several months trying desperately to beat extreme tiredness a friend of mine suggested I go and get some blood tests done.
"Well it couldn't do any harm could it?"
So off I went to see my family doctor.
It's probably just stress or depression", he said, "but I will send you for some blood tests and see if anything shows up."
Later that week my appointment came around and fasting bloods were drawn for analysis in the morning.
At 3pm I got a call from the Nursing Practitioner at the surgery "can you come into the surgery right away? Doctor wants to see you... your glucose levels are too high."
Oh Boy! I knew immediately what that might mean and half an hour later I arrived at the surgery feeling very nervous.
My fasting blood glucose was 23.1 mmols. At 4pm my levels were still 12 mmols, I was packed off with a prescription for Metformin, a blood glucose monitor and a bunch of leaflets all about Diabetes.

And so I was Diabetic!

Over the next few weeks the medication was changed to Gliplizide which made me sicker than Metformin did. Then in October 2006 I was started on Insulin Therapy and oral medications were ceased.
12 months later I was the proud owner of an insulin pump.
Now I could seriously get my blood sugars under control, and I did.

My HbA1c when I was diagnosed was 9.8%, after 12 months it was 6.5%, and after six months on the insulin pump my HbA1c was down to 5.7%. These results were superb and I managed to maintain those numbers for the next 2 years.
My success was largely down to spending a lot of time in online Diabetes community forums and it was here that I learnt the most about Diabetes and how to manage it best on a daily basis. I would eat a pretty healthy diet, watching the carbohydrate values of the foods I ate and matching the insulin I was taking. Mostly my foods were Low Glycemic Index, which meant that they would digest slower and release the glucose slowly into the system. So no great big blood sugar spikes after my meals. Evenings were the most difficult, as I was more insulin resistant in the evenings.
On the whole I found Diabetes to be reasonably stable for me and quite predictable, as long as I was healthy and not stressed, and I ate sensibly.

May 2009.
I was having a discussion with JB who told me stories about cancer patients eliminating all trace of their tumours. He explained how they were taking Bicarbonate of Soda to help raise the alkaline levels in the body, along with a diet rich in Alkalising foods.
I had a few issues with eating certain foods like dairy, wheat and gluten, which gave me some uncomfortable symptoms.
I decided to research some more and then put it to the test on myself. I had nothing to lose and everything to gain. At the time I had no idea just where it would take me.
I decided to Blog my progress, my saliva levels were pH 5.0 and Dear Hubby had levels of pH 5.5.
We bought in some Bicarbonate of Soda and took it each evening at bedtime. A dose of a half teaspoon in 250mls filtered water, swishing around the mouth before swallowing.

Blog entry June 30th
The pH Miracle Diet.
I've been researching this subject matter for a couple of weeks now. JB is a Naturopathic Practitioner. He tells me that cancer patients have a great deal of success once the body has become more alkaline. An acidic body is more likely to become sick as the acid stores in the interstitial spaces between cells. Over acidity is difficult for the body to deal with itself and it becomes sick and tired. The cancer patients invariably have been able to fight off any trace of even very advanced cancers adopting this method.

I've read a book entitled 'The pH Miracle for Diabetes'. Written by Dr. Robert O. Young and Shelley Redford Young, authors of 'the pH Miracle'.

What I've read so far makes perfect sense to me, and I have decided to give it a go. My body keeps telling me that it isn't right. At 41 years old I shouldn't be feeling so many back aches, stomach aches, and generally unable to eat many foods because they make my body complain so much. Better just to go with the flow.

So far I'm at the *'order everything in'* stage, blenders and green powder and sprouting seeds were ordered yesterday. Oh and a water ionizer too.
Once the green powder arrives I can get cracking.
Dear Hubby has said he will do the first 2 weeks liquid feast with me. Poor fella! I don't know that he will stick to it as he loves his cheese so much!

The diet pretty much consists of green veggies.....green drinks...and more green veggies! Much of the diet is to be consumed raw too. Could get windy in the Jones household!

The pH levels are measured from 0 to 14. With 0 being Acid, 14 being Alkaline, and neutral at 7.0
The optimum pH levels I was looking to reach were neutral which would mean that my body would be functioning at a much healthier and normal level. If my body is functioning at pH neutral then all organs should be running normally and efficiently, including my pancreas and liver. Also mentioned quite a lot in my research is something known as adrenal fatigue, something that occurs when the body is subjected to far too much stress and high levels of Cortisol over an extended period. This would appear to be commonplace in modern times with our busy lives as we rush from one thing to the next like frantic ants. The pH levels then are a barometer for how well our bodies are coping with the external stress of work, family and social stresses.

Throughout the blogs I refer to the insulin pump delivering both **basal** and **bolus** insulins. An Insulin pump uses only one type of insulin which is short-acting, however the pump can also deliver very tiny amounts of insulin at very frequent intervals giving the user an overall long acting effect, this is known as Basal Insulin.
Bolus Insulin is short acting insulin that is delivered on demand when the user requires a correction or wishes to take insulin for food that is consumed.
The pump is able to deliver both ways, and is fully programmable depending on the users' requirements.

Blog entry 30th June
pH diet.....info before I start.
Here's some information on my current state of health before I start the diet proper.
Total insulin usage over the last 7 days is average 21.3 units per day.
Basal insulin is 9.9 units per day.
Blood sugars on waking and pre-meal are usually around 5.5mmols.
Body weight 66kg/146 lb/ 10st 6lb
My body in general feeling bloated, aching in colon, headache, back aches, spotty skin, blurry vision, prone to depressive moods (see-saw moods) crave sugary foods a lot, and sick of stodgy foods.

Oral pH level this morning was 5.0

Daily supplements I take now.
2000mg Fish oils (high potency)
2000mg Flax seed oil
1000mg Glucosamine Sulphate
10mg Vinpocetine
Vitamin B complex (sub-lingual)
also
30mg Sea Kelp (only once per week)
and 5HTP as needed for times of stress.

To clarify, I was taking the supplements to support my body in different ways. I had found that fish oils and glucosamine helped relieve pain in my knee, hip and ankle joints as well as give repair and maintenance qualities when I damaged ligaments through repetitive strain injuries, I was frequently troubled with a bothersome computer mouse 'claw-hand' which appeared when I had been overdoing the computing at both work and home.
I was taking Vinpocetine to help with 'brain fog', for some bizarre reason I found that some days I couldn't complete simple sentences, Vinpocetine relieved that symptom.

I took Sub-lingual Vitamin B complex to combat depression. Vitamin B deficiency is found to be common in adults with depression. Research found positive results when patients took vitamin B complex, and in many cases the patients were able to completely be weaned off their anti depression medication. **[Note: please consult with your health care provider before changing any prescribed medications.]**

Flax seed oil to help with bowel movement and provide omega 3's
Sea kelp for iodine
5HTP taken as needed to help with stressful periods of life.

Overall I would probably describe my health as 'okay', but in a 41 year old I felt that better health was something I could strive for. To put it in blunt terms, I knew I could feel better than this.

I had now started ordering the supplements and equipment that I would need to get me started.

Blog entry 2nd July
pH diet early days
I've got started....after a couple of technical hitches.... namely that the seller on eBay had some difficulty sending me the right invoice for the right amount of postage, hopefully the green powder and ionizer will arrive tomorrow now.
In the meantime my new blender and food processor has arrived and I've been busy experimenting with the fridge full of green veggies.

The first smoothie was a 'design it yourself coz you're smarter than the book' disaster!
I blended a whole grapefruit, half a cucumber, some mint, a stick of celery and some water and ice-cubes. Blitzed the lot! Unfortunately I'd read somewhere that the white inner skin of a grapefruit is healthy so I left that bit on, minus the pips and zest. It made the whole smoothie very bitter, so I won't be doing that again. Better to play safe with grapefruit segments or juice only in future!

Dinner last night was an avocado salad made with a host of green veggies and peppers and big tomatoes. The salad dressing was made from the juice of a lemon and olive oil, gently flavoured with salt, chilli pepper and some herbs. I really enjoyed it.

I can't see me sticking to liquid only for the first 2 weeks as the book says. I will stick to it better if I can have an occasional 'real meal' too.
On the whole I'm quite happy so far, and of course because the smoothies are working out very low carbs I'm not taking insulin for meals at all. This will be monitored though.

The pH miracle book recommends starting out on green smoothies. Consuming only what they term a 'liquid feast' for the first few weeks.
The idea with this is that whilst your body is repairing itself you feed it with nourishing, natural, living foods that are easier to digest.
I was prepared to do this, and started looking through all of the recipes for green smoothies within the book.
My reason for not taking insulin with these 'meals' was that I had always been able to eat raw vegetables with virtually no rise

in my blood sugars at all. Fruit was off limits on this diet as it would cause a raise in blood sugar levels, with the exception of non sweet citrus fruits (lemon, lime and grapefruit)

Blog entry 3rd July
pH miracle part one.
Well I have to say after my initial (terrible) experiments with the smoothies, I'm starting to get the hang of the recipes. Dear Hubby has taken a long disgusted look at my blended cocktail of green veggies and doesn't fancy going on 'Gruel'!

My insulin requirements (for food) on this diet are nil, yesterday I did have a bag of potato crisps when we went out for a walk as I felt so weak and feeble!
My blood sugar levels have kept at a very respectable 5.0 mmols throughout until late this morning when I felt my blood sugars crashing down into the 4.0mmols region. I've now reduced my basals between 9am to midday on the pump so hopefully that will help with the drop there. There was a tiny drop there before but as I was having a good lunch I never did anything to correct it on the pump.

The parcel with the ionizer and the green powder still haven't arrived yet so I am limping along without them, a note from the postman tells me a parcel is waiting for me at the sorting office...fingers crossed that's it!

I made a delicious smoothie this lunchtime.
1 avocado
around 400mls almond nut 'milk'/soya milk (unsweetened)
a tablespoon of coconut flakes

blend it in the liquidizer and serve.
I also added some linseeds but that may not suit everyone's taste,
(I drank mine straight away but a squeeze of lemon juice would stop the avocado from browning)

I was already feeling weak and lethargic, and my initial thoughts were that my body was undergoing a deep cleanse and therefore detoxing. Not knowing how long this would happen I continued my efforts.

Meanwhile we had been taking the Bicarbonate of Soda for around 10 days.

Blog entry 4th July
pH diet part two.
Today I am very excited, a huge discovery has been made.
Hubby and I tested our pH levels using the new pH strips that arrived yesterday. Testing the saliva on the inside cheek when we woke up we both tested at pH6.75 !!!
Thinking that it was the new sticks we also tested using the litmus paper we used before, the paper revealed a lovely green colour indicating close to pH 7!!!
I'm so shocked that the change has happened so quickly. Neutral pH is 7.0

I have started the green powder which also arrived yesterday ~ to be honest it smells like something out of the bottom of a hamster cage! I'm taking half a teaspoon of powder with a pint of water, I can't say I care for it but if it's good for me and supports me with the right nutrients then I am willing to keep going with it.

I started taking a Chromium supplement; its job is 'to increase the effectiveness of insulin, improving its ability to handle glucose.'

Yesterday I spent the day chasing blood sugars in the 4mmols again all day. Low blood sugars are being treated with either a smoothie or carrot and some nuts. I'm still not taking insulin for meals as they are so low in carbs.

Overnight I've reduced my basal insulin by 10% (temp basal now 90%) blood sugars were still 4.0mmols when I woke up. Thank goodness I reduced it!

I shall maintain the lower basal today and monitor closely.

Dr Young (author of The pH miracle for diabetes) writes that your insulin changes will occur within the first 3 or 4 days.

My body feels less stiff today, my back is definitely feeling free, although the headache hasn't shifted for a few days, perhaps the headache has to do with release of toxins from the system. (I had similar ones during acupuncture treatment years ago whilst clearing liver toxicity)

All in all I'm quite enjoying the green smoothies.

Here's what I had for breakfast.

half large grapefruit (remove skin and pith and seeds)
handful of sprouted seeds (alfalfa, clover or others)
handful of fresh spinach
third cup fresh ground flaxseeds
1-2 tbsp Udo's oil (I used olive oil)
2 cups chopped broccoli (raw)
half cup chopped cucumber
1and half cups water

blend in liquidizer on medium speed, or high speed for smoother blend.

Serve and enjoy!
I enjoyed half of what I made, and then I was full up so kept the rest in the fridge until lunchtime.

My main worry by now was that I was taking external insulin and clearly my body needed less insulin than I was giving it.

When too much insulin is given the body uses up all of its glucose reserves, when the glucose reserves are too low then a hypoglycaemic episode ('hypo') occurs, in cases when more insulin is in the system than glucose the body can go into a coma or even death. The body is unable to function with no glucose.

So as long as I was feeding my body with external insulin then I had to test as often as possible and to make sure that I wouldn't go into a hypo.

I was testing up to 13 times per day.

As you will see I would reduce the amount of Basal insulin on the pump to balance the insulin/glucose levels.

The 'temp basals' I refer to is a setting on the pump that could be used to either increase or decrease the basal dose levels in 10% increments. So 90% temp basal means that I had programmed the pump to give me only 90% of my usual Basal dose.

Blog entry 5th July
Blood sugars during pH diet.
I've spent 2 days chasing what many Diabetics here would term to be superb blood sugars, and after meals there has been no noticeable elevation of blood sugars at all! I'm still not taking insulin for meals either. Please notice that I had a broad bean salad lunch yesterday which was a deliberate act to raise blood sugars up to a more healthy feeling. I feel so shaky and wobbly throughout most of the day. I did feel better after raising the blood sugars a bit. I ate nothing further for the day and blood sugars came down quite a bit until bedtime so I dropped the basal by another 10% to 80%.
I will keep a very close eye on things for the next few days.
Blood sugar report as follows:

2nd July
21.25   5.0mmols

3rd July
06.53   4.7mmols
11.45   4.3
15.23   4.6
17.15   4.8
19.20   5.6
21.55   4.1   reduced basal to 90%

4th July
06.15   4.4mmols
09.25   4.7
11.19   4.4
12.50   4.6
14.30   5.9
15.32   6.5
16.43   5.3
18.33   5.4
20.53   4.6   reduced basal to 80%

5th July
03.30   4.4mmols
06.55   4.7

Hubby and I are visiting JB who is very surprised at my body's quick response to the changes in diet.

Hubby and I both take bicarbonate of soda (half teaspoon in a little water swished around your mouth before swallowing) JB told us it helps to neutralize the acidic phase of the body which occurs during the night. He feels that the bicarb could be the main instigator for all of the changes. i.e. the body was being neutralized even before I started the dietary changes.

With so much going on it's difficult to tell what is doing what, but something is happening.

The green powder drink still tastes vile but I am persistent with it. And I am relieved to hear JB say that 4 litres per day is far too much liquid so I only have to drink 2 litres per day. He said something about drowning out vital electrolytes in the body with too much fluid intake.

We are off to a vintage car race/rally today with a few hills. Emergency nut bar in my bag and reduce basals again before I go I think.

In 5 days I had reduced my basals by a total of 20%, that's one fifth of what I was taking when I started out on this diet. Not forgetting that I was no longer taking insulin for meals and no need for corrections of high glucose readings either.

Blog entry 6th July
pH diet ~ 6th July update
Yesterday I allowed myself a nice dinner of Tabbouleh made with Quinoa, I had about a serving spoon portion with some broccoli and cauliflower and a nice piece of baked salmon. It was delicious! I took no insulin with the meal which I calculated would be around 30g carbs. 2 hours later my blood sugars were only 5.7mmols!!! I was ecstatic!!!!
Sadly the same didn't happen at breakfast or lunch today, but that's okay. I've made the decision not to take insulin for any meals and just correct if I need to at the 2 hours point, just in case the pancreas decides to kick in again.
Blood sugars report:
5th July
03.36   4.4mmols
06.55   4.7
08.47   4.9
10.10   5.2   reduce basals to 70%

12.00	4.7	carton apple juice 20g
13.40	6.2	
15.19	4.7	
17.09	4.9	
21.13	5.7	

6th July

02.41	4.1mmols	
05.00	4.6	30g quinoa for b/fast
08.19	8.0	
10.03	6.2	
12.01	5.4	bag crisps 20g
13.33	8.5	
15.19	5.8	
16.46	5.7	suspend pump for golf
18.32	4.6	
19.46	4.9	end golf ~ start pump

The basals have now been reduced by 30% in just a few days of starting this diet, at the moment they seem stable at the new rate...this is being monitored well.

I seem to recover quickly from any shaky episodes if I have some salt. I make sure to put sea-salt in every meal, it seems to be a really important ingredient. Must be to do with minerals and trace elements I guess.

The green powder drink which tastes vile seems to be improved in flavour by the addition of a squeeze of fresh lemon juice...hurray!

I'm getting the hang of the smoothies now and turn out some pretty good tasting ones, although they are better served in a bowl and eaten with a spoon. Tomorrow I will test the pH levels to check my progress.

So at 6 days in to the 'diet' I was enjoying remarkable results!
My decision to take no insulin with my meals was clearly working for me. I maintained a very watchful eye on my blood glucose readings, just in case of a sudden fall into those hyperglycaemic readings.
I most certainly didn't want too heavy a risk of going into DKA (Diabetic Keto Acidosis) which is very dangerous and potentially deadly.

Blog entry 7th July
pH update ~ 7th July.
pH levels this morning were:-

Saliva ~ 6.5
Urine ~ 7.25 (neutral!!!)

I appear to have developed cystitis though and apart from drinking loads of water I don't know what else to do with it. The traditional cranberry juice is off limits as its acidic fruit.

Blood sugars overnight have been stable:
7th July
19.46	4.9mmols
22.46	4.7
01.22	4.2
06.56	4.3

Basals are still running smoothly at 70%.

Blog entry 8th July
pH diet ~ 8th July.
Yesterday was a better day for me all round. Dear Hubby and I spent the day working together. The work involved lots of digging and wheel-barrowing. I did the barrowing; it was hard work, as my body still isn't up to full strength yet with the changes on the diet. I reduced my basals down to 20% for the purposes of the work load for the day.

7th July
06.56	4.3mmols	
12.02	4.8	
16.05	4.1	
22.19	4.0	

8th July
01.59	3.8	
05.08	3.3	carrot juice
05.37	4.5	
06.39	5.4	

I think the basals may be looking for a reduction again, so I will monitor blood sugars carefully today. Today will be another day of barrowing with Hubby.

The cystitis still lurks, I'm still resistant to using cranberry juice. I'm using some Russian technology called a Denar machine which works a bit like a needle free acupuncture kit. (Developed for astronauts) it seems to be helping to ease the symptoms. I still think it's happened as part of the change to alkaline. Dr Young (author of the pH diet for diabetes) explains that urine of diabetics is usually found to be quite acidic.
JB has suggested taking 'Bearberry' Uva Ursi so I will see if I can get some of that online today.

I'm reading through some of the recipes that follow on from the liquid feast phase of the diet, some sound really quite delicious and make tortillas using sprouted grains, the tortillas are not cooked but dehydrated and eaten in the raw state. It sounds interesting but also expensive, as you need to buy a dehydrating piece of kit to do it. More research needed here I think.

I know many Diabetics would kill for readings like these but I always felt that my glucose monitor gave me higher readings than my old monitor. Apparently blood glucose meters do vary quite a bit.

Blog entry 9th July
pH diet ~ 9th July.
Yesterday saw the advent of further reduction in basals! I'm astonished to say that my basals are now 40% lower than when I started this diet about a week ago! I still don't take mealtime bolus doses and don't need any corrections for highs either.

The diet itself is very low carb its true, but I don't attribute my carb intake to the changes in basals. Something more is going on here. I don't profess to understand, I just like the results.

Hubby and I were digging and barrowing again yesterday, my blood sugars plummeted even though I put a temp basal of 20% on the pump (thank goodness for the pump during these quick changes!) we worked until about 12 o'clock, I reset my basals to 70% but 2 hours later I was heading low, so set 60% basal where it stayed.
Overnight blood sugars dropped a little, I think a further reduction may be occurring in basals today.

We are mixing concrete today so more shovelling and barrowing for a couple of hours, I've already popped temp basal of 20% into the pump until I finish work.

Blood sugar report:
8th July

06.39	5.4mmols	
10.30	4.1	carb snack
12.01	6.8	
13.23	3.9	basal to 60%
16.23	5.3	
21.22	4.9	
23.00	4.6	

9th July

04.00	3.9	carrot juice
06.54	3.7	more carrot juice

Cystitis still affects me, the Bearberry that JB suggested is in the post, and hopefully it will arrive today. Apparently it is great for inflammation within the kidneys and bladder etc. so I'm hopeful that the tincture I've ordered will work quickly.

I checked out the food dehydrators, they start at around £75 but the bigger ones are more suitable for the types of foods I will be doing, they start at around £200 ! ouch!!!!!! I may have to talk nicely to Hubby!

Overall I'm very happy although mornings are difficult as I feel so ill when I move around. I've put that down to lots of changes taking place within the body and it will settle down.

So on day nine I have already reduced my insulin requirements by a staggering amount! And to also see the need for a bigger reduction during periods of physical activity is very promising and gives me an indication of what else is coming as I proceed on this amazing journey.

The apparent bladder inflammation seems to have been brought about as a direct result of alkalising the system.

JB suggests that the acidic waste is leaving through the kidneys and bladder and he isn't surprised that I am experiencing symptoms.

Blog entry 10th July
pH diet ~ 10th July
Overnight blood sugars prompted yet another drop in basals! Quite honestly I don't know how I would have coped on MDI! [Multiple Daily Injections] The beauty of a pump is that you can change basal rates at the drop of a hat.
So now my basal rate is running 60% lower than ten days ago when I got started on this diet!

Blood sugar report:
9th July
06.54	3.7	
12.00	4.2	Reduced basals to 50%
16.10	3.8	carrot juice
16.51	6.0	
22.20	4.6	

10th July
02.40	3.7	carrot juice,
02.40		reduce basals 40%
06.32	3.9	

It was a friends' birthday yesterday. We treated her to a nice meal out and I was pleased to be able to have a prawn salad without any dressings on it at least I could have a meal with her on her birthday.

Strangely I don't feel drawn to cheat on this diet, I am enjoying the reductions in basals and feel positive that perhaps my pancreas may be trying to jump start itself again after 3 years.

Hubby is concerned that I may be starving myself by not eating often enough and has encouraged me to 'graze' more often so that I get the maximum nourishment out of my food. What he says makes sense, I mean I have only been eating every 4 or 5 hours with the odd mouthful of almonds during the day. As we know salad is made mostly of water so doesn't last very long in the digestive tract!
He says I should take a big salad/veg box when we are away from home so that I can snack with no problems.

Today I feel a little better. I admit to have been feeling weak and washed out of energy this last week, and just put it down to all of the changes. This morning although it took effort to climb out of bed I feel a little brighter, and I get a day off from the heavy workouts as I am am awaiting a delivery of a bathroom for one of our customers, so lucky me I get to potter around the house munching lettuce leaves and cucumber.

We still haven't received the water ionizer from the seller yet, apparently it's been more popular than anticipated and they ran out of stocks! Delivery by the middle of next week they say.

I found a stockist in UK for Stevia, and ordered some yesterday so I eagerly await its arrival so that I can satisfy my sweet tooth again.

Hubby and I are talking about raising some cash to get the food dehydrator that I would like, the Excalibur is supposedly the best one to get, and it's also the most expensive. I want to make dried crackers and tortillas from sprouted grains mixtures as I think they might be the snack solution I am looking for.

I am pleased that the fall in my blood sugars has been reasonably steady. And that has enabled me to reduce my basal rates at a steady and manageable rate too.
Even so to be only taking 40% of the basal insulin I took 10 days ago is virtually unbelievable
If I hadn't been experiencing this for myself I may have had my doubts. How could someone's body respond like this and so quickly too?

JB was monitoring my daily blogs with anticipation and helped with a guiding hand where it was needed, that was an enormous boost for me.

Blog entry 11th July
pH diet ~ 11th July
The last 24 hours have been much quieter and my body now seems to be settling into its new dietary routine.
We had a golf lesson and played a couple of holes yesterday afternoon, it was fun, my game is improving, but after hitting a total of 100 balls my body was very tired, and my arms and legs went heavy.

Hubby agreed to let me order the Excalibur food

dehydrator, so I will be able to make chewy and crispy recipes that are made with raw foods. The dehydrator works by very slowly blowing warm air over the foods which are on trays. It dries the food without allowing it to turn to a fungal mess (YUK!) and without cooking it either.

The Stevia arrived this morning and I can't decide what to make using it, some people are never happy!

Blood sugars remain stable on the 40% temp basal

10th July
12.13   4.9mmols
14.50   4.8
16.00   4.9
21.03   4.9

11th July
02.25   4.1mmols
07.51   4.1
11.21   4.2

My body looks like it's lost a lot of weight, Hubby says I lost weight too, to be quite honest I was never overweight but just a couple of pounds off makes me look so svelte.

I'm contemplating trying some wild rice for dinner tonight with some fish I caught recently and popped in the freezer, along with a fine array of vegetables too. I nervously tried some raw zucchini/courgette yesterday and it's really yummy, so more of that for dinner tonight too!
I don't know what effect the wild rice may have on my system, so I will only use bolus insulin as a correction if my blood sugars go up. My portion will only be about a tablespoonful.

By now I was getting quite adventurous with my new raw food menu.

Blog entry 12th July
Now taking only 30% basal insulin!
Wahoo!! Today I feel so good with this alkaline diet. Today is the 12th day on it and I have seen such dramatic drops in my insulin needs I am bowled over!

This morning I tested pH levels in urine and saliva. Saliva is now pH 7.0 (started at pH 5.0 two weeks ago!) Urine is pH 7.2

I've lost 6 pounds in weight.

I tried a small portion of wild and brown rice last night for dinner, along with a nice piece of grilled fish and loads of the usual raw veggies, topped with a dressing made from lemon juice, olive oil and herbs/pepper. It was absolutely delicious. The rice portion was only about a tablespoon in size.
(On the alkaline diet I can have wild rice/quinoa/amaranth type of grains in small portions)

Blood sugar report:
11th July
07.51	4.1mmols	
11.21	4.2	
16.53	4.7	Rice meal no insulin
18.45	5.9	
19.53	5.5	
22.00	5.0	

12th July
00.05	4.9mmols	
05.23	4.3	rice meal no insulin at 6am then golf
08.11	5.6	

So the rice pushed the blood sugars up a tiny bit, but at 2 hours I think 5.9/5.6mmols after both meals is very reasonable indeed.
I'm thinking that the basal had something to do with it. In view of the drop from dinner to breakfast I have reduced the basals to 30% TBR on the pump now which is astonishing!!!!

Looking back over these last 12 days, my body has had quite a big job de-toxing itself, it's no wonder I felt so awful for quite a few days. I don't regret it though as

I feel marvellous and my strength is really coming back online now too.

If you remember I started out on an average daily TDD of around 22 units of which 9.9 units were basal.
Yesterday my TDD was only 5.0 units and nearly every day looks like that too.

TDD is the total amount of insulin taken in any given day.
A tablespoon of wild rice/brown rice was around 30 grams of carbohydrates. White rice and modern grains are not helpful when trying to adjust your bodily responses. The increase in blood glucose levels happens much quicker and so gives your pancreas a real jolt.
JB was advising me that ideally the pancreas cells reproduce every 56 days. Optimum effects could probably be seen if the pancreas was rested and not 'challenged' for that period.

Blog entry 13th July
So tired today....but still buoyant!
Hubby and I took a couple of our friends for a nice walk into the Welsh mountains to Cwm Idwal yesterday, it was a lovely day and we had packed our various lunches, mine was a box of sliced up zucchini, cucumber and bell pepper, I had what my husband terms my 'nosebag' of almonds as well which I munched on all the way around the lake. When we got home I collapsed into the sofa and could barely speak as I was so tired out! Zero energy left!!!

I always considered myself fit and quite capable to do these walks, in fact I had been to Cwm Idwal before and it is what I would term an easy mountain walk. Our young friend hates doing anything that involves effort and she did it (with constant complaining until we fed her with a sandwich!!!)
We both did it though!

Today I feel like a wet rag, my body is so tired. I wonder if my body is searching for sugar/carbs to get energy from instead of using fats to burn for energy. One of the main ideas about this diet is that your body gets trained to do just that...burn fat for energy instead of sugars.
I'm craving chocolate like mad today....monthly must be

lurking somewhere I reckon, all I want to do is eat. I will work through it though. Today I weigh 9st 13lb, a drop of 7 pounds so far. I didn't do this for the weight loss though, I want to get my body into a healthy state again, and it hasn't been healthy for a very long time.

A lot has had to change in my body, and is still changing. All of the cells of my body are changing. It's what I asked for and exactly what I am getting, a disease free body. A tall order?? Perhaps not.

Hopefully the soy sprouts powder will arrive today, I'm hopeful that they will inject some more life into the old girl, and I will start to feel more sustained energy. The soy sprouts powder is said to have oodles of protein as well as being packed with tons of nutrients. I sure hope it fills the gap.

Blog entry 14th July
Let the real meals begin!
Today a new turning point dawns.
I decided to include some small amounts of grains into my diet at least a couple of times a day. I can't stand being so tired all of the time.

Yesterday I felt so exhausted until I had an elevenses meal which included some wild rice and salad. Well let's just say I perked up straight away!! Although still a little tired and my body still feels like it belongs to someone else but at least I know I'm getting close to the right balance for me now.

Blood sugar report:
12th July
05.23	4.3mmols	Basal to 30%
08.11	5.6	
11.00	5.2	
13.00	5.0	
21.31	4.8	

13th July
06.33	4.1mmols	
08.30	4.6	
11.33	4.8	Rice meal, no insulin
13.01	5.2	
19.07	5.3	
22.01	4.8	

14th July
06.31   5.2mmols
06.31   buckwheat meal no insulin
08.11   5.7
09.53   5.7

So overall I seem to have reached a plateau again, I still think more reductions will occur, just a bit slower than the first lot!
The readings are all well within my normal parameters, with no need for corrections in either direction, which is very good!!!

I couldn't fight my need for something sweet and found a nice alkaline recipe for coconut freezer balls, sadly I didn't have all of the right ingredients in and thought I would have a go anyway. So I substituted the tahini for peanut butter (acidic food!) and the coconut oil for rapeseed oil (acidic). I enjoyed the bread-crumby mixture very much, although it didn't set as a solid block like in the recipe of course.

Curious to see what impact this snackathon would have on my pH levels I tested my saliva first thing this morning.... it's gone down to pH 6.5.......DARN that sweet tooth of mine!!!!! I shall have to work double hard to get it back down again now so that proves to me that even a small deviation from the alkaline diet will knock me back in these early days. Clearly my body is still adjusting.

Blog entry 17th July
Who said diets are boring!!! Hah!
This week has been just so busy! Hubby and I have hardly had time to turn around.
JB has suggested that the cystitis symptoms and extreme tiredness may be attributed to a lack of amino acid L-Lysine,
Wiki quote
L-Lysine is a necessary building block for all protein in the body. L-Lysine plays a major role in calcium absorption; building muscle protein; recovering from surgery or sports injuries; and the body's production of hormones, enzymes, and antibodies.

Lysine can be found in meat products, dairy, eggs..... basically all of the foods that I have stopped eating!

Typical!
It is also found in a number of beans and lentils which I do eat in small amounts.
I shall take a supplement for a while and see how it goes. As we have no Lysine in the house I've taken L-Carnitine for a couple of days, and also had a couple of egg meals. The cystitis symptoms have almost disappeared completely, and the tiredness is just tiredness now and not 'hit a wall' exhausted! I shall get Lysine tomorrow when we go shopping.

Blood sugars have been very steady, lowest 4.4, highest 5.8, with only a very tiny drop in basals overnight.

Meals continue in the alkaline tradition, mostly raw with the occasional cooked meal, even the grains I choose to have small amounts of are alkaline (buckwheat, wild rice, quinoa). Believe it or not I am actually really enjoying the menu.

The water ionizer arrived on Wednesday, we are very pleased with it as the water tastes...well...so *clean*!

And the Excalibur food dehydrator arrived to take up permanent residence in the kitchen too! Our kitchen is tiny so it's taken some creativity believe me!!!!

I filled the Excalibur up with some home-made vegan burgers, sliced tomatoes, courgettes, and a load of sliced garlic which we bought a load of the other day really cheap.
The result?
The house stunk of garlic, but the veggies were pretty tasty, ditto the 'burgers' which I have been snacking on today. YUM!

Just one more thing....the soy sprouts powder arrived this week, we got 90grams for £44 !!! The pot looks so small especially when you remember how expensive it was!!! I take it sparingly. The pH miracle diet book tells you to put it into everything....not likely at that price!!!!!!!
I'm sure I can manage just fine without it next time!!!!! I wonder if the pot is gold plated..........

The water ionisier filters out chlorine and other nasty chemicals, increases important minerals like magnesium and zinc, it has a pH neutralizing effect on our standard tap water AND ionizes it too. ALL ROUND GOODNESS!

Blog entry 19th July
Amino acids.
On JB's recommendation I finally got to the shop to pick up some L-Lysine yesterday, I have been so darn tired since I started the alkaline diet.

I took a dose of L-Lysine with dinner last night and another with breakfast this morning. Hubby and I played 8 holes of golf this morning and I haven't felt better in ages!!!! With only a small trace of tiredness in my muscles!

Last night I tried some sprouted wheat bread which was on sale at the health store, I had 2 small slices, it tasted really very sweet, not unlike a malt loaf, I did check the ingredients and it said the only ingredient was sprouted wheat, my blood sugars promptly bumped themselves up in the 8's!!!! So I had a correction dose of insulin to bring it back in line again!

Most of my meals have included some buckwheat these last couple of days, if my blood sugars rise at all then they promptly come back down by themselves. Pre-meal blood sugars are still 4.5 to 5.5mmols.
This morning I awoke with 4.3mmols, had buckwheat, avocado and blended mix of veggies for breakfast, checked my blood sugars before golf which was 6.5mmols, then 2 hours later after golf (with pump suspended) blood sugars were back down to 5.5mmols.

Insulin usage is so small now, average daily TDD (total daily dose) 3.7units, compare that to the 23 units TDD averaged when I started.
Basal insulin is still steady at 30% of my previous basal. The pump has been marvellous for managing insulin basals during my first couple of weeks of changes.
Saliva this morning is pH 6.8

Buckwheat, Quinoa and Amaranth can be enjoyed as a raw sprouted vegetable if you don't fancy the boiled grain. It is much more of a protein food than its cooked carby version and so packed full of goodness.

Sprouts are easy to grow on a window ledge in your kitchen too.

Blog entry 20th July
Had a nice meal out.
Last night Hubby and I treated ourselves to a nice meal out. We have been working every day for the last 2 weeks so it was high time we allowed ourselves some slack.

There is a nice hotel in Beaumaris that we like to go to, it serves bar food, and we always enjoy our meals there.
So Hubby had his usual veggie dish, and I chose the Greek salad which comes served with mini Naan bread. It was delicious! We followed that up with a sweet each and then found an ice-cream parlour on the way home and enjoyed one each there too! We pigged out and had lots of fun on our 'date'.

I decided one meal won't kill me (a little of what you fancy) and this morning I'm back on track with a cleansing breakfast smoothie made with all of the usual greens, the same thing will be served for lunch, and a monster green salad for dinner tonight.

More amazing still is that my blood sugars showed signs that a further reduction in basals is in order so my pump is now set to only 20% TBR (temp basal rate).

I am staggered and again very pleased that this has happened! I didn't think it was going to come down so quickly!

I didn't take any insulin for the meal out last night as I wanted to see if my body would deal with any of the carbs I had challenged it with. So at 9pm I took 2 units to bring my blood sugars back from 9.8mmols down to 4.5mmols. This morning blood sugars were a neat 5.0mmols ! And that's with the new 20% basal too!

The bladder has decided to act up again since starting the Lysine, while I'm not tired anymore my bladder has presented me with constant urgency to use the loo. Uva Ursi to the rescue again!

JB suggests that a spike in blood sugars of 9.8mmols after a hearty meal would possibly have been quite normal in a non-

Diabetic person, so with that in mind I may not have needed the insulin correction at this stage.
I was just playing safe here!
With regard to the bladder inflammation flaring up again, JB tells me that the quick re-balancing of the amino acids is at play here. The bladder may well have been affected by an over load of L-Arginine compared to L-Lysine. Ideally they should be equally balanced. JB maintains that taking the L-Lysine will help to sort things out.
Well I am willing to try anything. After all this whole diet was an experiment to see what would happen, so far I have everything to gain and nothing to lose.
I believe quite strongly that the benefits outweigh the pitfalls so far.
I just love feeling so good!

Blog entry 22nd July
20% TBR still holding.
Overnight blood sugars are still stable on the new 20% basal rate.

Its interesting to look back over the last 3 weeks, the journey has been incredible, and challenging. But I do feel quite normal again now, and the cystitis symptoms are easing with the use of herbal supplement Uva Ursi 3 times daily.

Under JB's suggestion I've now added Alpha Lipoic Acid to the regimen, it's supposed to increase insulin sensitivity. Unsure how soon to expect any changes I will keep a close eye on my blood sugars again.

Saliva pH levels this morning 6.5

Blog entry 23rd July
I'm excited!!!!
Dinner last night was some sweet potatoe, part-cooked Broccoli, avocado and a host of raw salad/veggies topped off with a dressing of olive oil, lemon juice, fresh chilli and some Indian spices. It was delicious!
I wanted something sweet and I caved in and munched on some chocolate hubby had stashed away. It was half a bar of a dairy free chocolate that I like. A full bar is 27grams carbs. I took no insulin for dinner or the

chocolate, preferring to correct later on if I need to.

Half an hour later I tested my blood sugars

22nd July
18.25   8.2mmols
21.15   6.1
02.45   5.3
07.45   5.6

How neat is that??

Blog entry 26th July
The good work continues.
The last couple of days I have been able to replicate the raised blood sugars with carby foods (rice) and then watch in amazement as my blood sugars then reduced themselves slowly but surely down to 5.2mmols.

23rd July
02.45   5.3mmols
07.45   5.6
20.30   5.6
22.25   6.0
23.55   6.2

24th July
07.10   5.9mmols
11.55   5.7
14.15   4.8
19.00   7.5
21.55   5.2

25th July
05.35   5.6mmols
08.10   7.2
10.10   5.4
12.40   6.4
15.10   5.0
18.30   6.7
20.00   8.9
21.40   8.5
22.20   7.9

26th July
05.45   6.3mmols
08.32   6.0

So as you can see things are pretty stable, any increase in blood sugars was purely down to eating carby foods.

I pushed things a bit more last night and had a 20g portion of dairy free ice-cream after a 30g rice dinner. The blood sugars shot up in half an hour to 8.9mmols, I resisted the urge to take insulin at this time and watched my blood sugars slowly decrease overnight. This morning I awoke to blood sugars of 6.0mmols. I've just topped up with a tiny bit of insulin to bring those suckers back into line. I figured a little insulin might prompt my own production to remember what it's supposed to be doing.

You may be looking at my food choices here and see that not all of them are alkaline now. The bulk of the diet is. I do allow myself something of a break occasionally too now that the detox is complete. The diet book says you can eat acidic foods now too if you wish but keep them to only 20% of your diet and eat as much as possible raw. I don't eat meat at all but I wasn't enjoying eating it anyway. I still eat fish though.
Breakfast this morning was a 'vegan scrambled eggs' made with crumbled firm tofu flavoured with turmeric and ginger, lightly stir fried with chopped onions and, a handful of kale and served with avocado, cucumber and tomato.

I'm still puzzled by the cystitis symptoms, and why do I have the bladder capacity of a walnut??? Hubby suggested that the lemon juice may be irritating the bladder. The symptoms are easier again this morning since I didn't have any lemons at all yesterday. My urine this morning is pH 7.3 !!!! Its neutral!!!!! Wahoo!!!!!
Saliva is only pH 6.5 though. Could be because of the ice-cream last night perhaps??? I shall have to toe the line a little more me thinks.

The Alkaline diet would probably be best as a ratio of 90:10 (90% Alkalizing to10% Acidic foods) during the early stages to allow the body to fully restore itself.
Then a maintenance level of 80:20 or even 70:30 once a more balanced pH neutral has been achieved.
I keep being told that the pH of human blood is ALWAYS pH 7.45 and so it is impossible to vary that at all by eating a special diet.
I understand the key to this diet is that the blood draws all available nutrients from other parts of the body to maintain its

rightful balance. Does this then not leave your internal organs/ joints and bones in a state of imbalance?
I'm no scientist but I know what has happened to my body is no wave of a magic wand!

Blog entry 29th July
Food for thought.
I guess the biggest question here would be how on earth do I find variety in my diet to keep me interested enough to keep it going indefinitely?

This is a diet that has turned me into a rabbit food munching vegan hasn't it?? You would be forgiven for thinking those very thoughts, yet each day I manage to excite my taste buds with something new.

This morning's 'smoothie' has been made from a few simple ingredients which all get blitzed in the blender.

1 avocado
handful of kale
handful of spinach
250 ml soya milk (organic/unsweetened)
tablespoon of dried coconut
handful of dried almonds
juice of half a lemon
pinch sea salt
tablespoon olive oil
half teaspoon dried ginger

sounds gross doesn't it?? Yet it's so creamy and almost like porridge, and despite the light green colour.
It's absolutely delicious. I make variations of this every morning, and as it makes enough for 2 servings I will finish it off with some crunchy veggies dipped in it for lunch... Yum!!!

The last couple of days have seen a very slight increase in blood sugars. My pre-meals and fasting blood sugars have all been around the 6.0 mmols mark, I've put it down as being stress related.
The carbs in my meals are all still without insulin, and generally blood sugars come down in just a couple of hours, with the exception of the Sunday roast last weekend! I couldn't say no to those roast spuds, Yorkshire pud, apple pie and ice-cream. And I felt like c**p the next

day for it too!!! Days like that serve to remind me why I stick to healthier choice foods. My body doesn't like western foods...even if my taste buds do!!!

Serves me right! But it's prudent to point out that treats are not the end of the world. Just pick yourself up and make the next meal really alkalizing to make up for it.
Of course challenging the pancreas so often is not good, I should have really been behaving myself!

Blog entry 1st August
Now this is living healthy!
Today heralds a full 31 days on the pH miracle/ alkaline diet for me.
I still feel marvellous, I am eating better than ever before, and have even started buying raw food 'un-cook' books. I still experiment with the Excalibur food dehydrator hubby kindly purchased for me.
The first couple of weeks were definitely the worst, but then my body was undergoing some serious detoxing, I felt like I was being re-calibrated!

On a daily basis my blood sugars are holding steady at around 5.5mmols both fasting and pre-meals. I haven't eaten any 'white carbs' for several days and don't feel I need them at the moment. I'm not craving anything either. I don't miss eating meat at all. The only animal protein I eat now is the occasional fish. Hubby and I also enjoyed boiled eggs for breakfast a couple of days ago, I teamed it up with some toasted gluten free bread (normally off-menu) I enjoyed it but at the end of the day I felt so tired. I can only think that going back to eating cooked foods is having that effect. I like feeling alive. And I can only do that by eating live foods.

Hubby and I went out for a short walk the other day, about 20 mins we thought.

An hour and a half later we had walked right out of the forestry and onto an island that is attached by the beach. We explored the island and we then realized we had to walk back to the car!!! We reached the car again after a very brisk hour and 10 minutes walk, feeling elated and tired from our fun adventure. And my blood sugars after such a long walk?? 5.2mmols.

As you can tell in this entry I was feeling great with a capital 'Gr'!

I was noticing however that my efforts in the Excaliber dehydrator were having a rather flatulent effect and I would feel quite bloated. I tried some shop bought dried fruits which had the same effect too!

Now I know that other users have also had this experience.

If you can try out some dried food goods PRIOR to committing yourself to an expensive kitchen gadget like this one. Although the machine was really good, some peoples digestion really just can't hack it.

Blog entry 6th August
I'm doing so well here!!!
Five weeks into this new way of life.
I still can't believe I have come so far in such a short space of time.

I've spent 3 days with no basal insulin at all. I've totally taken off the pump now. Although I do carry my novo pen around just in case I need a correction while I'm out anywhere
apart from one correction last night after a 45gram carb dinner. I've not had any other insulin in 3 days. It's amazing. (I could have miscounted the carbs for dinner thinking back now. But even so my blood sugars only went as high as 7.7mmols. Not bad at all for a Type 1 who had no insulin with dinner heh???)

Tonight is another experiment, I've had 30 grams of rice and a 10 grams of fruit salad for my meal along with the customary salad and avocado. I hope that my blood sugars will reduce suitably before bedtime. (fingers crossed.)

The oral pH levels are still holding at pH 6.75 ~ that's first thing in the morning before drinking or brushing of the teeth.

I haven't taken the Super Greens drink for 2 days now and I can honestly say I don't feel quite right in myself although I am still strong enough to hike up mountains and then play golf. Yeah I know some people are never satisfied.

P.S.
Almost forgot to post that my blood sugars are so stable that they hardly stray off from 5.2 - 5.7 mmols even after eating !!!! Wahoo!!!

The results of my evening meal experiment were blood sugars that went up to 7.9mmols and then dropped back down to 5.2mmols at bedtime.
30 grams of carbohydrates was my 'limit' before anyway. Also my body responds better to carbs during the day.
If I eat carbs in the evenings my blood sugars are much slower to return to normal, plus eating my evening meal before 6pm helps.
Hubby nearly fell over when I told him I had removed my pump. We had just finished a round of golf and with blood sugars of 4.8mmols at 6pm I announced that I hadn't worn my pump since 9am that morning!
He would have been so worried, but I had tested every hour to monitor my progress.
As my daily total insulin (TDD) was only 2 units daily now I calculated that my blood sugars shouldn't raise that dramatically without any external insulin present.
So monitoring my blood sugars hourly I was able to detect any slow rise and therefore the potential need to provide basal insulin or indeed any correction insulin of it was required.
I would just like to add a note here to say that I wouldn't recommend stopping taking your prescribed medications without consulting your medical team first.
[ALWAYS SEEK THE ADVICE OF YOUR MEDICAL TEAM BEFORE ADJUSTING YOUR MEDICATIONS.]
I was confident and very carefully monitored my progress throughout, studying the effects of foods and insulin on my body all the way through my journey.

Blog entry 10th August
It's progress and it's good.
It's been almost a week since I turned off my pump, and opted for the 'no insulin unless I really need it' regimen.

So far its working, my pancreas has been well behaved and I only get blood sugars that refuse to come down from 7.9mmols when I eat more than 30grams within a couple of hours.
Most of the time my blood sugars don't leave the comfy zone of 5.3 to 6.2 mmols. I believe that is considered to

be 'normal' blood sugars for a non-D. My fasting blood sugars are invariably 5.5mmols.
Any corrections I've taken have been about 1.5 units in any given day.

This morning my fasting blood sugars was 5.9mmols which is a little higher than my normal one, but 2 hours after my breakfast smoothie blood sugars had come down nicely to 4.7mmols.

The 2 hours point was what I was looking for. Up to now my blood sugars have been taking up to 4 hours to come back down, and I was hopeful that the pancreas would remember how it should work and kick in to proper function.
I suppose I could describe this like a young bird trying to take off, at first he would bump along flapping his wings until suddenly a gust of wind would lift him up in the air. I am still monitoring very often, but I remain quite calm and confident throughout.

Hubby and I are seeing quite a bit of stress in our life at the moment, although my blood sugars don't appear to have risen like I had expected. To compare...when I took my driving test last October my blood sugars shot up to 12-14 mmols and I was taking a raised basal until a couple of days after taking the test. So again it would appear that my body is normalizing itself.

All in all, I really can't complain at all, I am really pleased and remain quite confident that I am seeing a long term effect here. My pancreas appears to have re-booted itself, and I'm still confident that this is all as a result of my choosing only alkaline or alkalizing foods. I've been eating this way since around July 1st and I would think that I will be choosing this way for the long term as well.

Blog entry 12th August
Test with control group.
My wonderful sister-in-law was volunteered to do a study with me comparing blood sugars for a day this week.

She is non-diabetic and I am a reformed recalibrated type 1 (non-dependant).

Here's what happened:

Time	Notes	Sharon	Diana
07.30	Breakfast	5.9	4.9
10.45		4.7	4.6
13.00	Lunch	5.0	5.3
15.00		5.2	5.8
18.00	50g carbs	4.7	5.2
20.10		11.3	8.2
21.05		5.4	5.9
22.30		5.4	5.8

Actually the evening meal was more like 19.00hrs so the 11.3mmols reading was as my blood sugars hit the high scales, but look at how quickly it came down!!! We had wild rice and red quinoa served as a delicious Tabbouleh.
No external insulin was taken at all during the test period.

Come to think of it, I've not taken any insulin at all since last Saturday evening! As I write it's now Wednesday afternoon. Wahoo!!!

Since I did the test period with Diana on Monday, my blood sugars have remained fabulously stable with no big rises at all, this is still early days, but my blood sugars seems to stay between 4.3 and 5.5mmols now. So my averages are much lower too. I'm bursting to know what my A1c will be! Also the c-peptide results!

I'm very excited!!! ....can you tell??

Blog entry 13th August
Fabulous!
My numbers are still marvellous. I've been adding fruit to my diet gradually these past few days with no bad effects on my blood sugars at all. The fruits I'm eating are of course all alkalizing.
Mango, banana, strawberries, and apple.

While my diet is largely alkalizing I do eat around 20% acidic foods now as well. Once the detox was done, and my blood sugars and insulin settled I was able to start to add some of the acidic foods, so I really don't feel like I'm missing out.

When we are away travelling or on the go I can usually find a salad from somewhere and have had chicken or tuna with it even some mayo too!

I do really enjoy this way of eating, I always liked vegetables and healthy eating anyway, although I wasn't over fussed on the salad thing, I eat salads made up to include my favourite raw veggies, so each meal is fun. I love avocado, and the salad dressings I make just enhance each meal for me.

Last nights' dressing was kind of like a pesto I suppose.

half a cup of sunflower seeds
juice of 1 lemon
olive oil
half fresh chilli pepper(including the seeds)
Braggs aminos to taste (a soy sauce)
teaspoon fresh ginger (or to taste)
tablespoon of desiccated coconut

Blitzed in the blender until smooth, or less time if you prefer it chunky.
Serve with dinner or use it as a dip for crunchy chopped veggies.

My saliva levels are still pH 6.75 this morning, I also woke up with a sore throat today, I hope it doesn't develop into anything really challenging. Blood sugars were fine at 5.7mmols so will wait and see.

Blog entry 13th August
12 Alkaline Foods to Revitalize and Energise Your Body.
This list was taken from an Australian website, it isn't exhaustive, and in my experience differing lists do vary a tiny bit, and with some foods your body may respond differently.

1. **Raw Almonds** soaked overnight produces a lovely juicy 'fresh' nut which can be used to make 'nut butter' or nut 'mylk'
2. **Fresh Green Leafy Celery**
3. **Sour Cherry**
4. **Fresh Asparagus**
5. **Fresh Organic Tomatoes** surprisingly Alkalising – more so when eaten raw.

6. **Raw Spinach** – use in salads or smoothies
7. **Tofu** - baked or stir fried
8. **Cauliflower** steamed or grated and eaten raw
9. **Whole Potatoes** – baby new potatoes steamed or baked jacket potatoes or sweet potatoe grated raw or baked
10. **Raw Carrot**
11. **Artichokes**
12. **Broccoli** steamed or small florets eaten raw dipped into an fresh green soybean dip which is delicious

There are of course many other foods that play a major role in the alkalizing diet.

Lemons for instance are highly alkalizing, added to your drinks during the day will help you to reach that pH target, also make vinaigrettes using lemon juice, Olive oil and your favourite herbs and spices and drizzle over any of your meals.

Avocado is rich in amino acids as well as those all important fats that keep you fuller for longer. Try adding it to a smoothie for a rich and satisfying meal.

Sprouted lentils, seeds and beans add a nutritious snack right from your own window ledge! Add them to your salads and smoothies too!

Blog entry 14th August
Surprised today.
It's been 6 weeks now since I began the alkaline journey.
Recently I have noticed that my face looks a different shape. So I jumped on the bathroom scales this morning and discovered that I now weigh in at 9st 10lbs.
I started out weighing 10st 6lbs.

I know I wasn't overweight to start but I didn't think I would lose more weight after the initial 6 lbs loss to boot!

The sore throat was pretty sore again this morning, I'm treating it with a type of acupuncture machine, as yet my blood sugars are still perfectly normal at 5.2mmols fasting.

I had a calf muscle cramp during the early hours, not sure what caused it yet. I do take sea salt with most of my meals. I am a bit puzzled.

My weight finally stabilized at 9st 10lbs, so my weight loss was actually only 9lbs in all.
I do feel much better for it and I have noticed much better muscle definition since eating this way too.
I have seen raw vegan athletes who look marvellous and so toned too so I figured its more about the healthy eating lifestyle that I have now adopted. I wasn't this toned or muscular when I was much younger so it must be my diet teamed up with the work I do with dear Hubby.
I am obviously rather pleased with this result.

Blog entry 15th August
A meal with friends.
I just can't believe my blood sugars are so stable, and I keep pinching myself thinking I will wake up any minute...!

Hubby and I were invited to join our friends for a meal at their house last night. We had a lovely time catching up and enjoyed the meals that they had prepared for us.

For starters we had homemade leek and potatoe soup.

For me they had baked a chicken breast with tomatoes and mushrooms, and sautéed potatoes and onions. There was a big bowl of salad on the table as well so I had a big portion of that too. Everyone else had veggie lasagne and garlic bread.

That was followed up with a portion of dairy free ice-cream served with fresh summer berries, they even blended some to create a yummy sauce over the top as well.
It was delicious!

Well obviously my carbs count was starting to run away with me so I wondered what my blood sugars score would be at the 1 hour then the 2 hour points. In total I reckon I had approx 90grams carbs! Wow I haven't eaten that heavily in weeks!

So after 1 hour I tested and even though the display on my meter is not working correctly I'm sure I saw it read 9.8mmols (gulp!). Then at 2 hours it read 5.4mmols!!!

Tadaaaaaa!!!!!!!

My pancreas rose to the challenge and worked its magic even after all of those carbs!!!!

I don't suppose I would want to eat like that every meal now, I do like my veggies and now I've got my veggie smoothies off to a fine art too. I'm still excited though! And quietly patting myself on the back for my hard work and dedication.

Oh and the best bit, my fasting blood sugars this morning were 5.0mmols.

Very neat indeed.

It would be nice to be able to eat meals like that every day, but I know from experience now that my body soon rebels and puts up the red flag.
So for me at least, hearty meals must be kept in moderation if I am to continue to see those low fasting and post meal blood sugar readings.

Blog entry 16th August
Diet transition thoughts.
As you probably know by now I don't do things in halves! The alkaline diet was 'jump in feet first and just keep paddling.'
Well it certainly paid off even though it was difficult to start with.

It is possible to make the changes at a slower pace though, that way perhaps we are more likely to stick to our new found diet and reap the rewards of our success for much longer.

For me there is no question that this diet works for me, I won't be going back to my old ways in a hurry that's for sure.
The quality of the foods we put into our bodies certainly has an impact on how our bodies respond, as diabetics we all know this well.

So what would I recommend?

First port of call is definitely **Bicarbonate of Soda.**
Taking half a teaspoon each night at bedtime in plenty of water (swish it around your mouth before swallowing) This helps to neutralise the acidic phase your body goes through each night and goes a long way towards making your body more pH neutral.
Everyone will respond differently to this supplement but it does work.

Dear Hubby didn't do the diet with me, but he stopped taking coffee, no more soda drinks and he cut down his cheese intake to only one portion per day [instead of 3]. Taking bicarb seems to have helped a lot as well.
The sores he was getting in his nose are history (probably down to the reduction in cheese) and he feels much better in himself. His pH levels rose from 5.0 to 6.5 in around 10 days. I feed him sensible meals, he is veggie so there's plenty of nutritious goodness on his plate each meal as well.

Now if we could just get my stepdaughter to eat some greens......!

Taking a slow start into the diet would probably suit many people, too much change too soon = a diet that you wouldn't stick too... or benefit from.
However just adding more and more raw and alkalizing foods to your regular diet and you may be surprised at how much and for how long you would see a change for the better. A new lifestyle choice, no more diets. Choose healthier.

Blog entry 17th August
Another day in paradise?
Last night I had some buckwheat for dinner with the usual veggies and a nice 'raw' sauce poured over it. It was really quite tasty.

I had the (hormonal) munchies a bit later on so I ate a packet of plain crisps.

Of course I'd forgotten I had eaten rather a lot of buckwheat around 50grams, so followed up with the crisps of 27grams it was quite a hefty meal.

My blood sugars at 9.30pm were 9.8mmols. Oh C**p!! I set

my alarm for 2 hours later and blood sugars had dropped to 6.1mmols, my fasting blood sugars this morning were 5.4mmols.

Good job Pancreas !

The sore throat is still there, it's a bit tonsillitis-ish (my tonsils were removed at age 17), still not had a chance to get any colloidal silver spray which has been recommended to me. So the acupuncture machine is still being used. It certainly helps anyway.

Blog entry 17th August
Spicy raw tomato sauce.
I really enjoy trying out new things on my food. Well just plain salad doesn't really do it for me. I like to eat lots of flavours and feel full after my meal. I served this over my plate of curry flavoured buckwheat, salad and steamed veggies last night. It was delicious.
<u>Ingredients</u>.
3 tomatoes
half fresh red chilli, use the seeds as well if you're brave!
1 avocado
a dash of Braggs amino (or soy sauce)
tablespoon of olive oil
juice of 1 lemon
tablespoon of sunflower seeds

blitz it all in the blender until smooth then serve.

Blog entry 5th September
My progress.... update at 9 weeks
Hello all!
I'm still going strong on the alkaline diet, and it's been nine weeks now in all.

I'm enjoying the food, lots of experimenting and finding new ways to prepare and serve foods that interest me. Keeping me interested will keep me doing it for longer right??

I would say 90% of my diet is alkaline and raw.

Blood sugars

I'm doing extremely well, lowest reading has been 4.3mmols,
highest was 8.8mmols.
fasting blood sugars are around 4.6 - 5.3mmols.
my average blood sugars are around 5.6mmols
and my standard deviation is around 0.8, an awesome improvement on an earlier calculation of 1.4, so my endogenous insulin response overall is much better.

Insulin.

I last took insulin for a correction of 1.5 units 3 weeks ago. We had eaten out and I succumbed to the fries and rice that arrived on my plate with the sweet potatoe and spinach curry. It was delicious. I took no insulin for the meal, and at 4 hours blood sugars had stuck at 8.8mmols. Hence the correction. Many Diabetics here would be in awe of such a low number after a massively carb loaded meal though so I am thankful for the small rise.

Prior to that correction I had taken no insulin for 2 weeks.
So one dose of insulin in five weeks!!! Pretty impressive huh??

I feel good, and friends who haven't seen me for a few weeks are saying I look different....in a good way.

I look and feel so healthy.

Additional supplements

To support the pancreas during this time I have included:
Chromium Picolinate
Alpha Lipoic Acid
and Vitamin D3

Experiments

I tried a few food experiments,
Fresh fruit is on the menu now, no serious rises there.
Boiled baby new potato ~ no probs if I stick to around 30grams.
Rice noodles ~ no can do! Blood sugars went up to 8.8mmols with only 30 grams worth. (tried that one twice)
Brown rice, keep to only 30grams with no probs.
Amaranth ~ yummy (like a savoury semolina) can eat 30 to 50 grams no probs at all here.

Basically the alkaline foods list seems to be dominated with foods that you can eat raw, if it needs cooking it's not as alkalising.

I still eat 10% of my diet as slightly acidifying foods, I have the odd egg. I've totally gone off meat. Fish has appeared less and less too.
I love tofu, and all manner of beans, so my plate is pretty much vegan these days.

Favourite foods
Green smoothies eaten most breakfasts and lunchtimes.
Lots of nuts (soaked almonds)
Fruit ~ Bananas/apples/kiwi/watermelon/strawberries (about 2 portions daily)
and oodles of green veggies, especially spinach!

So what more incentive do I need to stay on the alkaline diet ?? I have good health once more.

Blog entry 9th September
A raw foodies daily menu.
Okay so you've heard me spout off about eating alkaline, and eating raw etc it is true I have chosen to eat this way, and I actually enjoy it.
The results of my efforts are fantastic to say the least, 'standard deviation' is more like 'hardly any deviation' as my blood sugars barely rise up above normal non-Diabetic values. And fasting blood sugars are just amazing.

So I thought a sample menu might help to explain how I 'do it'.

Breakfast
Green smoothie.
handful of raw broccoli or kale
handful of raw spinach
250ml soya milk
juice 1 lemon
third of a cucumber
half a cup of sprouted sunflower seeds
2 tablespoon olive oil
sea salt
1 avocado

I eat half of this for breakfast

lunch
I eat the other half of the breakfast smoothie for lunch, sometimes with chopped raw veggies to dip in.

dinner
I choose from either
salad
this is made up of grated cauliflower, raw spinach, tomato, cucumber, sprouted sunflower seeds, grated or baton raw carrots, sprouted raw quinoa, avocado.
top that off with a dressing made with olive oil, lemon juice, fresh ginger, fresh chilli, Braggs aminos (like soy sauce)

or
raw zucchini <u>noodles</u> (sliced on a mandolin) topped with finely chopped tomatoes/peppers chilli/ginger/soaked almonds, served with basic spinach salad.

or
if I fancy a cooked meal, then lightly steamed broccoli/cauli/peas and soya beans with spinach salad
or
the steamed veggies with stir fried tofu slices.

pudding (yes even pudding!)
handful of frozen strawberries, one medium banana and some almond flour. sometimes a little soya milk.
whizz it in the food processor until smooth....and enjoy soft homemade ice-cream!

snacks
I eat a lot of almonds! I get on better with them if I soak them as they give me a sore belly when I eat so many.
Once a week I make raw food crackers in the food dehydrator. They are great to snack on or use for dips. The ingredients for the crackers are generally zucchini, carrot, nuts and lots of flavours. There's very little in carbs in these little fellas!

I've not gone 100% raw, but I would say 90% is raw, and definitely more and more of my diet stays in the alkaline brackets too.

I know this diet would seem controversial to most people, and wouldn't suit everyone either. But I am weird and I like the diet and I like feeling healthy too.

I forgot to mention that we like to eat out occasionally too, and I have found places where I can have a Greek feta salad with some baby new potatoes which doesn't affect my blood sugars at all.

Blog entry 15th September
10 weeks alkaline update.
I'm sure many people thought I wasn't going to stick to this diet. But as I have reached the 10 weeks point I find myself craving raw foods, and craving alkaline foods most often.

Gone are the carbohydrate cravings for biscuits, fries, pasta and bread.

Hello to the fresh food.

Hubby and I laugh at our 'His' and 'Hers' refrigerators. Mine is full to brimming with veggies, fruits and soya milk, Hubbies is full to capacity of soya yoghurts, cream and custard, some cheese, and his fruit/carrot juice.
He has stuck to his non-raw/normal diet, although he has swapped his menu for less dairy, no coffee and no soda drinks. His saliva levels are still maintained at pH 6.5. They were previously pH 5.5 before the changes.

My own levels remain constant at pH 6.75 now, they were pH 5.0 previously. I have increased my bicarbonate of soda each evening to try and raise this a bit more. I feel that such a good alkaline diet should push my pH levels towards more alkaline at some point. Initial changes were very rapid indeed....and then some!!!!

I can see that I will stick with this diet for the foreseeable future. What can I say?? I love the results of my hard work.

My weight is stable, my blood sugar levels are in non-diabetic ranges ALL the time now.

Because they are so stable I only test 3 or 4 times daily now. Although I do get a thrill seeing my non-diabetic numbers.

I've had to include some eggs back into the diet lately as I get tired for no apparent reason. Eggs would seem to have all of the magic ingredients that will remedy that, so I am eating around 2-3 weekly. Eggs are actually off the alkaline menu as they are said to have an acidifying effect. But I feel that I need to listen to what my body needs and provide nutrients accordingly.
I've always been better at that.
Brown rice is back on the menu too (cooked of course). I had been eating more raw veggies and less cooked grains, but it's the same story as the eggs, they have vital nutrients that I need right now.

I find myself questioning how I will stick to a raw/alkaline diet when the season changes and the supermarkets stock mostly root veggies (which are off menu), and how will I manage when avocados are over £1 each when I currently pay £1.19 for a 4 pack now!
I think lots of spring greens and steamed leeks will be on the menu. Also it's lucky I like raw Brussels sprouts! Yep sliced up and served raw with onions and garlic. All I need to do is work out a nice dressing to go over the top of 'em too!

All in all I can recommend trying this diet to anyone, take it slowly, and give it a go.

Blog entry 24th September
Eating out on a Raw diet.
It's been 12 weeks now, I still love the diet although my meals are currently more cooked than raw, but that's okay as they are alkaline. And I'm off my smoothies at breakfast, choosing a salad instead. How our taste buds change heh??

Hubby and I have continued to take the super greens powder as a drink each day. I take it up to 3 times. It's how I would imagine pond water would taste, but you do get used to it. And it's so full of goodness so it's an important part of my intake daily.

Body weight
My start weight was 10st 7lbs,
now I weigh 9st 9lbs and holding.
My body seems to have found its 'happy' weight now and I feel good.
Friends are noticing that I have lost 'loads of weight', let's face it I wasn't over weight before so that weight loss really notices.
It is a happy by-product of the diet.

Eating out.
We like to eat out sometimes. The main problem I'm having is finding places that serve nice salads that aren't covered in cheese and meat. Local restaurants don't understand the term 'vegan' and you end up with a plate of vegetables that are tasteless!
Last night I ended up ordering a chicken Caesar salad (that's really all there was to choose from for me).
When the meal came it was loaded with big slices of bacon. Grrrr. I thought it would have tiny pieces that I could leave to one side, but the bacon definitely outnumbered the chicken by 2:1 and I felt cheated!

Blood sugars
My blood sugars are still holding in the fabulous non-diabetic way that I am becoming accustomed to, after eating carbs my blood sugars diligently make their way back down to normal after a couple of hours. I'm still so chuffed to see them do that.
I only test around 3 or 4 times daily now. Just to keep an eye on things.

My fasting blood sugars are slightly raised although still under Diabetic parameters. This morning was 5.8mmols. Stress appears to be affecting only the fasting numbers, and only a little.

Diabetes Tools
I've been logging and tracking my blood sugars on a

diabetes tools package which has proved to be quite useful in looking for patterns. I get the odd spike when I've been naughty, or eaten something with 'blind' carb values in it. Most spikes are around the 7's mmols region (normal non-Diabetes values.)

A 'smoothie' served at pizza hut at the weekend gave me a spike of 9.8mmols! The highest I've spiked since I started! I was quite disappointed and haven't eaten any carbs since to make amends. The smoothie must have had some form of syrup added to it.

I'll stick to the water next time.

Blog entry 28th September
Review bloods are booked.
3 months into the new diet I've now announced to my GP that I would like a C-peptide as well as the standard HbA1c. He looked puzzled at first but on hearing that I no longer need to take insulin after 3 years dependence he agreed....after picking his chin up from the desk that is!

The earliest date/time available for fasting tests is next Monday morning. Uh! A long wait!

The doctor asked me when I am scheduled to see the diabetes clinic/endo, which isn't until next May some time. He suggested they may wish to see me much sooner when we see what my results are.

Quite honestly I didn't expect that kind of reaction from the medical world, I expected more of the 'explain it off' routine that I have become so accustomed to.

But, it's all good, and what a morale boost!

Blog entry 9th October
A carby experiment....
Overall I've been doing pretty well on the new eating regime and I thought a night off and some tasty treats were in order.

So hubby and I decided to enjoy the company of some of our friends and invited them for a dinner party last night.

We served prawn cocktail for starters with a slice of

wholemeal bread (homemade of course.)
Main course was Camembert and cranberry jelly in filo parcels for our guests, and stuffed cabbage leaves for me with veggies and some vegan cheese-a-like that I bought recently.
The main course was served with roasted Mediterranean veggies and boiled new potatoes, topped with lashings of hubbies famous tomato sauce which he makes with oodles of white wine, mushrooms and courgettes, basil, etc
I just had a couple of potatoes and some veggies with my cabbage wraps.
Pudding was served....gluten free apple pie, dairy free vanilla ice cream and whipped soya cream. All homemade (except the cream). It was heavenly!
I declined the alcoholic beverages.

Total carbs consumed I reckon on around 80grams.

I tested my blood sugars an hour after the meal finished.... Gulp! 9.9mmols!

I tested at 3 hours..... Oh dear I thought as I read aloud 8.8mmols.

Hubby awoke this morning and thought I was dead as I was so still and he had to put his hand on my belly to feel me breathing.
....he worries about my high blood sugars and not taking insulin for them.

...I was fine.
and the best bit is that my fasting-post-carby-meal-blood sugars were 4.6mmols.

Today I've been craving food like it's going out of fashion and my blood sugars are still slow to come down after a meal. So I guess I'm not cured yet lol.

I'm gonna have to get back into the green smoothies again for sure. I just can't face them much right now since the weather has turned colder.

Each time I eat large amounts my pancreas responds slowly the next day. A bit like a tired Athlete after a long run.
I'm still amazed that my body is still able to sort itself out though.

Blog entry 13th October
It's all about balance.
No-one is perfect, least of all me, but when the formula resolved a problem, the result has been to make long term changes to my lifestyle of eating.

'The pH miracle diet for diabetes' suggests that as a diabetic we should consume no sugars or white carbs at all. This would be to give our pancreatic cells the best chance of rest and potentially some recovery.
This I did for around the first 5 or 6 weeks. And in that time I did see very dramatic results in my diabetic and overall health.

No carbs was all well and good but it became apparent that my body needed some form of carbohydrates. I was always tired and totally lacking in energy.

I tried some quinoa, amaranth, brown rice and wild rice. In small portions of around 30grams carbs I found that my body functioned better and could sustain energy for longer periods without having to eat 24/7 to achieve this. And because they are non-glutinous grains they are considered to have only low acidifying effect on the body so eating them doesn't undo all of my hard work.
In fact quinoa and amaranth are also protein foods and rich in amino acids that support the body.
Baby new potatoes are also shown to be low alkalizing.

Other foods served alongside these grains/cereals would be heaps of salad and steamed veggies, thus achieving a pH balance that was generous on the alkaline side. I observed as my saliva pH levels went more neutral.

The percentage of alkaline/acid would be best at around 80:20, for many weeks I achieved a 90:10 split, I managed it well but really needed more carbs, particularly when I was to be physically active.

A dietary regime should always be about what works best for you, I know of several other Diabetics that eat raw foods in high quantities and have been able to reduce or cease their insulin or medications altogether. Some of them even eating only fruits!

My main staple foods on this diet are:

Lemons
Olive oil
Avocado
Apple
Spinach
Broccoli
Kale
Sweet peppers
Onions
Tomatoes
Bananas
Almonds
And of course my window box sprouts.

So to make up your alkaline percentages make sure your acidifying foods don't make up more than 20% of your plate.

Here's to a good Healthy Life.

Blog entry 16th October
New HbA1c.
I went along to the family practitioner today for my blood results. Lo and behold a power cut had left the surgery with no power and having no back up, the computers were all dead too. Oh joy!!

Doc was good enough to use his cell phone to contact the labs and get my HbA1c results. The C-Peptide hasn't come back yet as it gets sent to London for analysis.

In May my HbA1c was 5.8%
today it's.....
5.2%
I kind of knew that my HbA1c was in for a small drop but I was more interested on the C-Peptide/cholesterol etc etc.

So while I'm pleased with the reduced HbA1c I'm also disappointed that the other results weren't available too.

Blog entry 26th October
Results....
I'm 17 weeks now into the alkaline diet, so how am I doing??

Well my energy levels are more stable now than the initial few weeks. If I feel tired now it's because I've worked hard, exercised hard or played hard, sometimes all of those.

The diet is becoming much easier for me too, as I really do prefer green raw veggies to stodgy 'normal meals' now. And fresh fruit features a lot, especially apples and bananas.

My blood sugars are doing great, my morning fasting blood sugars that I posted recently are still consistent, and spikes are few and far between.

I still take vitamin D3, Chromium Picolinate and Alpha Lipoic Acid each day to assist the pancreas in its new territory. That's alongside the bicarbonate of soda each night.

My blood results came in from the tests I had done a couple of weeks ago.

HbA1c 5.2%
thyroid ~ normal
kidneys ~ normal
liver ~ normal
cholesterol ~ 3.8

We are still waiting for the C-peptide to come in. I hope it isn't lost.
So both my HbA1c and my cholesterol have reduced since commencing the diet. 1 more pound and I will have lost a stone in weight too. Today I weigh in at 9st 8lbs (starting weight was 10st 7lbs!)

And of course it's been weeks since I last took insulin for anything. The last dose was 23rd August.

I'm really pleased with my progress. My family practitioner says, 'it's nothing short of a miracle'.
My 'therapist' (JB) is thrilled as well. And of course I have the loving support of my adoring Hubby who watches over me constantly. What more can a girl wish for?

Blog entry 27th October
Raw ice-cream? You bet!
Here is the recipe for one of my favourite raw desserts.
Its all natural with no added funny business!

Take a cup of frozen berries (I love strawberries but any will do) and a chopped frozen banana and pop them into your food processor and pulse chop them until there are no big lumps.
Add a fresh banana and blend to make it really creamy, and serve!
Its creamy and delicious. Oh! ...and alkaline too!

I serve mine with either dried coconut or sprinkle cacao nibs for a really yummy dessert.

Blog entry 4th November
Update.
I've been chasing my family doctor regarding the results of the C-peptide I asked for.
It's been a few weeks since the bloods were drawn and I thought it must be back by now.
Anyway he phoned me up yesterday, he had contacted the lab at the hospital to find out what was going on, turns out the family doctor can't order a C-peptide.
He told the nice lady in the lab about my progress and results on the diet and she is fascinated.
And she has given the go ahead to order the C-peptide!
I had the bloods drawn today, they get sent off to southern England somewhere and the results will be back in around 8 weeks.

EIGHT WEEKS??? something to do with it being an expensive test and all.....

Blog entry 11th November
Dieting in 'real life.'
Finally we appear to have got back on line tonight. Our ISP has been having fault issues and we have been virtually on dial up speed for the last couple of weeks. Hence no recent posts. Sorry about that but when surfing becomes crawling and pages don't load.... well, you get the picture....

I've been enjoying a rather varied diet this last couple of weeks. The change of British weather conditions from 'wet and windy' to '*cold*, wet and windy' has brought with it a need for cooked meals that replace or complement the preferred alkalizing raw foods.

Hubby and I have been working flat out refurbishing a kitchen, dining room and hallway. So spending lots of time preparing meals hasn't been an option. In fact I admit to eating more than my fair share of shop bought healthy snack bars. The snack bars have made up around 20% of my diet so everything else should have been alkalizing to balance it out.

The day starts out with the supplements washed down with a pint of filtered water and a scoop of mega greens powder.
Then breakfast has been a cup sized portion of cooked brown rice, served with a medley of raw vegetables and topped off with sprinkles of pumpkin seeds or sunflower seeds and a dressing of olive oil and lemon juice.

Midmorning snack is a healthy snack bar (brown rice, fruit, nuts, seeds, carob, honey etc) the carbs are around 25g each bar.

Lunch another snack bar with an apple and a banana.

Mid afternoon snack if I'm hungry I will have another piece of fruit or snack bar.

Dinner is typically plate of steamed veggies or salad served with hummus or tofu.

Followed up with pudding, I make either a frozen fruit ice-cream or a low carb nutty/coconut 'freezer cookies' recipe.

Of course the above list makes me sound like a alkaline angel....which would be misleading....!

The other day I ate a bag of chip shop chips (fries). I have to report that my blood sugars didn't rise above 7.mmols all afternoon! And after 4 hours my blood sugars were 4.3mmols!

The next day I fancied one of hubby's teacakes with some

margarine on them, actually I ate 2 of them (gulp!). They were delicious but my stomach felt so heavy afterwards and my body reminded me why it doesn't get along with foods that contain gluten.
I have decided that although the fries and the teacakes were rather nice to my old way of eating, it really doesn't suit me to eat that way nowadays.

Curiously since I had the carb overload in the fries and then the teacakes my blood sugars have been superb! In fact today I had trouble keeping my blood sugars over 4.5mmols!

My pH levels are still holding at 6.5 even with falling off the wagon a little.

So diet? Yes **definitely** but with a little slack occasionally.

Blog entry 17th November
Patterns within patterns
As I analyse my relatively normal blood sugars these days I can't help but notice at least one pattern emerge in my fasting readings.

In fact to see them plotted on a line graph I can see quite clearly that the pattern looks like that of a gently bouncing ball.

That pattern coincides with my monthly cycle.

Mostly my fasting blood sugars will be around 5.0mmols to 5.3mmols, and for around 10 days before menses starts I see slightly elevated readings, here I will see 5.6 to 5.9mmols. Once my period has started I see my fasting blood sugars drop back into the lower range again.

So even in someone who has normal blood sugars there is a clear rise and fall during the daily scheme of things.

Meanwhile we are enjoying the company of our family whilst hubby and I are decorating their living room, and getting plenty of pampering and good alkaline foods whilst I am here.

Breakfast was a colossal bowl of fruit. In it there was 1 small banana

1 small apple
1 kiwi
a tablespoon of mango
1 tablespoon of pineapple
a chunk of chopped ginger
some olive oil
half juice lemon
sunflower seeds
raw cacao nibs
and sea salt

followed by a boiled egg.

It was absolutely delicious!!!!!!

I have found that I need more carbs in the morning to give me that boost of energy, also I take my pancreatic supplements before breakfast so I feel that they kick in pretty quickly too.

I've started reading 'the thrive diet' written by Brendan Brazier, he is/has been a top tri-athlete ironman who eats only living/raw foods. This is inspirational as I am looking for that edge that gives me sustained energy during my active times.

Blog entry 19th December
Alkaline Xmas
Hubby and I are heading off for a two week break to stay in a lighthouse over the festive period. We are being joined by various members of the family and also visiting with other family members, even so it should be a nice relaxing break away from the stress of everything.

My blood sugars are currently running on the higher end of my 'normal' range. Fasting this morning was 5.8mmols. Not dire straits but enough for me to keep a close eye on things.

Meals during the festive period will still be mainly alkalising in nature. Although I do plan eating a traditional Xmas meal minus the Xmas pudding! Also choosing more veg and less carby offerings.
I plan to enjoy myself.

This week I was approached by two sets of friends who

have decided to change their poor unhealthy bodies to pH neutral zones. I have been enlisted to help them.

I suspect this will be the start of my book writing.

Anyway before I ramble on too long, I would like to wish you all a very happy festive time. Be healthy and happy and choose well

---

Blog entry 23rd December
Holiday ouch!!!
We arrived at the lighthouse in good time before the snow fell on Saturday, it's great, we woke up to about 4 inches of snow on Sunday.
Walking around the cliffs in the snow was awesome, the snow had frozen and was twinkling in the sun.
Later in the afternoon we had been out shopping for groceries and I slipped on the ice, landing on the side of my ribs. Yep, I broke one of em!!! The pain was immense! I felt like I had been kicked by a horse for about 24 hours!
Things have settled down now, and I've been to the hospital A&E, had an x-ray and got some decent painkillers.
The most surprising thing of all was that my blood sugars didn't rise up much beyond 7.7mmols ! Hubby is looking after me so well, I feel so pathetic because I can't lift anything heavier than a cup of water! And I'm normally so independent!!!
I'm still determined to enjoy my hols and just taking everything really steady on the ice.

Blog entry 27th December
Healing nicely
Today marks 7 days since my rib injury, it's not been an easy week but today I felt much better and it is the first day I've not taken painkillers so I'm definitely on the mend.
Blood sugars have been amazing even despite being surrounded by yummy festive food!
Morning fasting blood sugars have been consistently 5.4mmols, I'm really pleased with that.
JB (my practitioner) has suggested I take a new supplement which will counter the stress aspect of my life, it's called DHEA. I'll find the appropriate info and post it later. So far though I am a cool cucumber and hormone activity is very settled too.

Blog entry 30th December
My New Year RAW-volutions.
As I reflect over the journey that shaped 2009 for me, I can't help but observe that diabetes management is so different this festive season compared to last year.... for me that is.

Xmas 2008 I had flu that knocked my blood sugars around so much I was still taking an increased basal dose of 140% until 3 weeks later!
This year I have had the seasonal bugs and barely noticed a difference in my blood sugars at all.
This year I broke bones in my chest and my blood sugars only registered up to 7.7mmols for the first day before levelling out. (No biggie huh!)

The difference between the two is that I eat differently this year.
I chose to eat more alkaline and more raw foods and to eat in a more natural way.

My body is more alkaline.
My body responds to diet and exercise and doesn't need external drugs or insulin to help it on its way.

Now, I'm no angel and there have been bumps along the way, and I do eat the occasional standard western meal or titbit.
But as long as I make the majority of my eating plan raw/alkaline my body continues to respond in a predictable way.

Its true! I love to eat raw foods!
My favourite right now is a really simple dish.

raw broccoli florets
raw cauliflower florets
raw spinach/rocket leaves
raw baby tomatoes
raw sweet potatoe sliced
sunflower seeds
raw whole hemp seeds
sesame seeds
cracked pink Himalayan salt

juice half fresh lemon
olive oil
sprinkle some herbs

That is the same formula for most of my meals, but I then I add one of the following

2 boiled/scrambled eggs
tablespoon quinoa/amaranth/brown rice
tablespoon of hummus

If I eat out then I choose a non-dairy meal, preferably veggie as well, but I do choose from salmon or chicken too. It depends what's on the menu really.

Mainly I stick to the menu whilst still watching out for those carb counts while I'm at it.

My body is still sluggish at responding to large carb amounts. I'm working on that.
I hope that once the family external stress thing is sorted out my pH levels will rise up and that last anomaly will iron itself out.

So on the whole 2010 is looking good. And I'm really proud of myself!

Blog entry 5th January
Free as a bird... and some science.
Finally after 18 months the stress inducer in our lives has now ended and we can finally continue to live our lives normally.......at last!
The reason I mention this is because it has had a considerable effect on the health of our bodies.
I've been monitoring my pH levels daily for a few weeks and noticed some interesting patterns.
Initially it was thought that my monthly cycle would be affecting acid levels but the rise in blood sugars with the cycle didn't have any direct effect on pH levels on its own.

Increases in stress however did have a direct effect and I noticed when I was particularly stressed my saliva levels dropped to pH 6.5. My saliva levels should be more like pH 7.2.

My practitioner suggested taking a new supplement called DHEA.

Taking DHEA had an immediate effect on my saliva levels, which suddenly shot up to pH 6.75 and stayed there, stress was much easier to deal with and I don't have much in the way of PMS either (must check that with hubby though).

Over the festive period my weight went back up to 9st 13lb, I had got down to 9st 5lbs before the festive break. Consuming more carbs has obviously had a knock on effect that way. Since we came back from our hols I have been making good and eating right again (I much prefer to eat raw veggies).

Blood sugars are lurking in the 6mmols area this week, my monthly is imminent I'm sure.

The rib is aching like mad, sleepless nights as I toss and turn trying to find a comfy spot. It's been 2 weeks since the injury so the bone must be knitting together well now. I can feel a lump now over the break. Perhaps the rib is affecting my blood sugars too?? Time will tell I think.

Overall I feel really buoyant today, and a great sense of relief that hubby and I can finally move on together in our new found freedom.

Blog entry 6th January
Normal....at last!
Yeah okay who is normal around here!

As I mentioned previously Hubby and I are now able to relax into our new lives together...free of the things that have caused us so much angst over the last 18 months.

I test my saliva pH levels each morning as routine now just to observe a pattern. Taking DHEA supplements definitely helped to boost the levels up to pH 6.75 when it had been stuck on pH 6.0 for weeks with the occasional nudge up.
However the morning after we finally shook off the stress inducer in our lives my saliva levels jumped up to pH 7.2 = NORMAL!!!!!

HURRAY !

That's two mornings on the trot that I have tested pH 7.2, actually this morning my results were kind of in between pH 7.25 and pH 7.5 did I mention that I am thrilled?

There is no doubt in my mind whatsoever that the alkaline diet has been a success for me.

As I type I am munching on raw broccoli florets dipped in red pepper flavoured hummous. Yummy!

Blog entry 13th January
Strange.
A couple of curiosities have arisen since my last blog. Namely that my fasting blood sugars are on the rise again for no apparent reason. The pattern over the last six months has been in the mid 5's mmols which I have been quite content with, however since the recent festive period and notable rib injury my fasting blood sugars are lurking around 6 mmols.

My saliva levels while I had achieved a very satisfactory pH 7.25 two mornings on the trot I haven't achieved it since and today I tested at pH 6.5 again. Humppphhh! Will I ever get the hang of this??

Rather than beat myself up over it there must be an explanation for this reduction in pH levels and rise in fasting blood sugars.

1. I've been taking regular doses of ibuprofen to ease the constant aching from the ribs as they knit together again.

2. Sleep patterns aren't regular as sleeping with afore mentioned rib injury is rather uncomfortable and wakes me up each time I turn.

3. Is Ibuprofen affecting the overall picture regarding pH levels?? I don't take more than 2 doses per day if I can help it, as I would rather manage without.

Given time, I will no doubt get to the bottom of it, in the

meantime I have increased my intake of alkalising foods and drinks to bring everything back into line again.

Blog entry 14th January
pH diet surprise.
Hubby and I have been doing the rounds visiting our friends and catching up with the news. It would seem that I am the news!

My friends remark on how lovely my complexion is (I rarely wear makeup), how clear and sparkling my eyes are, and how well I look in general. I would seem to have an inner glow. And of course I lost weight which is noticeable to those who we haven't seen us in a while.

I have been asked to help friends who have rather different diseases to diabetes, yet the pH diet is designed to assist ANY BODY to re-establish its natural rhythm and regain good health once more.

Blog entry 15th January
Back on track now.
Over the festive break recently I put on quite few pounds in weight, 7 pounds in fact ,mainly because we were eating out so much and eating raw and choosing alkaline was nigh on impossible when eating in that way so I just muddled through. I would choose alkaline when I prepared my own meals of course but those carbs still got through.

This last 2 weeks I have watched my weight come back down very neatly and I have lost 6 of the 7 pounds I gained already! I didn't starve myself to do that either, just chose my usual alkaline meals.
I've started to sprout beans and seeds again. This morning I enjoyed sprouted lentils on a bed of spinach and tomatoes, I did top it off with a couple of poached eggs. I can't ignore my cravings for foods like eggs, it seems my body needs the amino acid L-Lysine and eggs, whilst they are seen as acidic, but I should balance that with the needs for better body function all round., L-Lysine is also available from Quinoa and Amaranth, I am experimenting with the sprouting and soaking, many raw vegans rave on about the benefits of eating sprouted

grains so I will give it a try and see how much more beneficial it is to eat these grains in the raw so to speak. I would like to choose to eat 100% raw if I can, I see myself in transition to do that.

Saliva levels were back up to pH 7.0 this morning, great news indeed, and my blood sugars were back down to 5.4mmols too. I am much happier about that too.

So celebrations all round.......now where is that chocolate.......??

Blog entry 24th January
Bean sprout heaven
This week my fasting blood sugars are much more impressive, it would seem that sure enough as I suspected my 'monthly' was taking its own sweet time and messing my fasting blood sugars up good style.
Now it's finished I'm seeing average 4.6mmols each morning which is a vast improvement on the 6mmols I was getting. Don't you just hate hormones!

I'm still enjoying the Alkaline diet and my saliva levels are consistently pH 6.75 in the mornings.

Favourites right now are sprouted green lentils.
I soak an amount of lentils overnight, then rinse then thoroughly and drain well.
Rinse them with fresh water 3 times daily until they have little tails. I usually eat mine when they have reached about 8mm.

I'm a big fan of hummus but as it's not a 'raw' recipe I would really like to come up with a tasty replica that fills the alkaline/raw gap requires. So far I've had a batch of chickpeas go rancid on me as they took so long to sprout. Darn it! I really like sprouted chickpeas but they need to sprout green leaves before they are edible for my taste.

Sunflower seeds are really quick sprouters and they make yummy sunflower seed pate 'also known as raw/vegan cheese.'

Our kitchen window looks like a bean sprout farm!!!

It turns out that 'raw' chickpeas have a rather toxic effect on my body so I can't say I recommend them 'raw'.
Smaller sprouted legumes and seeds are much more digestible, less chance of them going rancid and they taste so good.
Alfalfa, horseradish seed, broccoli seeds, also lentils, adzuki beans, and mung beans lend themselves well to sprouting.

Blog entry 1st March
Help! the Carbs got me!!!!
I was doing so well.
I switched to a mostly Raw/Alkalizing diet last July '09, within 5 weeks I no longer needed insulin or diabetic meds.
My blood sugars have been near perfect all of that time and would only wobble when I challenged my Pancreas with Carby meals, the result was usually a sluggish Post Prandial (PP) which would be back to normal at 3 to 4 hours instead of the expected 2 hours.
I don't test too much these days, usually twice daily, fasting and bedtime. Fasting blood sugars typically are between 5.4 and 5.9mmols, bedtimes can be anything between 5.2 and 9.2mmols.
Hubby and I enjoyed a Chinese take-out meal with family over the weekend, I ate more rice than usual (about 75 grams) followed by about 6 prawn crackers (resistance was futile!!!) bedtime reading was 9.2mmols and fasting the following morning was 5.8mmols.
To be honest I've been eating more carby meals like that lately, I don't know why but I just had a magnet for carby input, I knew it was no good for me yet....... I still ate it!
Too many carbs!!! Not allowing the pancreas to rest and recuperate and eating way too much has taken its toll. I have also put on 6 pounds in a couple of weeks which I don't like.
Anyway palpitations several times this past week have reminded me why I started the diet in the first place and now I have started back on track in ernest.
And now I can tell the carbs...get thee behind me!!!!

And so my 'alkaline/raw' versus 'western titbits' diet ebbed and flowed, and my pancreas dutifully continued to meet with the challenges it was faced with. Still only taking the pancreatic supplements Alpha Lipoic Acid, Chromium Picolinate and Vitamin D3. The broken rib took quite a few weeks to heal before

it stopped aching, but once I got back into the physical building work with dear hubby, I quickly built quite a defined muscle tone and increase in physical strength. Recovery from injury was very quick and I generally feel aglow!
My weight is stable, barely fluctuating at all from 9st 10lbs.

Blog entry 4th March
A day in the life of the pH Alkaline Diet
I have been approached by a number of members here who wish to know more about the Alkaline diet, so this blog post is for you.

Today I have eaten.....

Breakfast
Glass of filtered water with 1 scoop powdered super-greens.
Salad - tomatoes, cucumber, spinach, 2 spoonfuls of lentil salad mix, 2 scrambled eggs. Dressing of lemon juice and olive oil. Sprinkles of sunflower seeds.

Mid Morning
Apple and banana

Lunch
Salad at Pizza Hut, included spoonful of hummus, coleslaw, tomatoes, lettuce, chillies, diced peppers, sweet corn, cucumber and half an apple. Topped with the low fat vinaigrette.

Mid Afternoon
orange and a bar of carob topped seed bar
cup of Miso.

Dinner Tonight
Grated raw sweet potatoe, raw broccoli and grated cauli, cucumber, baby tomatoes, chopped leek, spinach, topped off with a raw 'salsa' type sauce made with 3 sun dried tomatoes, 1 red bell pepper and 3 medium tomatoes, flavoured with a pinch of curry powder, a clove of garlic, a squeeze of lemon juice, dried basil and sea salt. Believe me it's delicious!!!

I may have a banana if I fancy a sweet, chopped up in a bowl and sprinkled with dried coconut and raw cacao nibs (raw cocoa).

Just to explain, the principles of the alkaline diet are that you should include only 10 - 20% of acidic foods to your diet once you have reached your target pH level (neutral is pH 7.0) [my saliva levels started out as pH 5.0 and are now between pH 6.75 and pH 7.0.]

The alkaline foods you choose to eat are more alkalising in their natural state, the more a food has been processed or cooked the more acidic it is.

This is the reason why the majority of my diet consists of raw foods. My experience has been that it suits me better and I do feel much better on the raw version. But if cooked is all that's available then I will eat cooked. (ie eating out or at friends house)

Some days I fancy eating carbs, so I will include a 30g carbs portion of either brown rice, Quinoa, Amaranth or Millet.
These grains are the least acidic and in some lists I have checked they are listed as mildly alkaline.

I enjoy sweet potatoe [cooked or raw] and occasionally baby new potatoes [cooked].

In case you missed my recent blog 'Help the carbs got me!' I wrote how eating off diet was detrimental to my blood sugars, now that I'm back on track eating the raw alkaline foods properly my blood sugars are awesome.

This morning my fasting blood sugars were 5.0mmols !!!! Hurray!!!! I've been struggling to get it down below 5.6mmols, so this is a real motivator for me!

A list of Alkalising foods and recipes can be found later on in this book

-----

Blog entry 6th March
Alkaline menu ~ Fri and Sat
I thought it would be useful to post each day what I have eaten so that readers may get some idea of how I stick to the Alkaline diet.

FRIDAY

Breakfast
1 Pint of filtered water with scoop of Super Greens powder.
1 Apple (10g)
1 Banana (10g)
Carob topped seed bar (19g)

Mid morning snack
1 small orange (5g)
1 Apple (10g)

Lunch
Salad with 2 scrambled eggs (0g)
1 banana (8g)

Dinner
Salad and Avacado (15g)

total carbs 77g

SATURDAY

Breakfast
Gluten free bread (26g)
2 boiled eggs
Salad (0g)

Lunch
half ripe Mango (10g)
1 Apple (10g)
1 kiwi (5g)
carob topped seed bar (19g)

Mid afternoon
1 Apple (10g)

Dinner
steam/stir fried celery, garlic, half red bell pepper, 1 cup of edamame (soy) beans (20g), half leek, half cup chopped broccoli stalk, 1 gluten free stock cube
1 cup raw cauliflower
1 cup raw broccoli
squeeze fresh lemon juice
half cup green olives

Total carbs 100g.

Hubby and I have spent the last 2 days working in our garden chopping trees and shredding them. It has been very hard work and today I felt so tired.
The eggs I have been eating have been to try and replace the lacking Amino acid L-Lysine, we have run out of the supplement L-Lysine and it is mainly found in red meat, eggs, brown bread and soya beans amongst other foods.

We took a trip out to buy some as the eggs weren't quite hitting the spot. I should be full of beans again tomorrow.

Once I went back onto the Alkaline diet properly my fasting blood sugars are looking really good. Today 5.2mmols. GREAT!!! (when I was eating off the diet my Fasting blood sugars went up to 7mmols one day which I wasn't happy about).
In fact my pre-meal blood sugars before dinner tonight were 4.3mmols, that's my lowest in weeks!

I am very happy to be back on track.

Blog entry 16th march 2010
Fasting blood sugar success!
2 days on the trot now I have had 4.8 mmols fasting readings!!! I was excited about reaching 5.0 mmols over the last week but this is just great. Now if it will go down a bit further I will be really impressed.

As well as sticking more to a raw diet where possible, Hubby and I are working quite hard on making our home bigger. So lots of barrowing for me, and digging for him.

I love getting stuck into the physical aspect of building and I certainly love the positive impact it has on my blood sugars!

I'm hunting for new raw food recipes that will inspire me. My meals feel a bit 'same-y', salad, salad, salad, salad..... I need something new!

Perhaps some raw vegan burgers made from sprouted lentils and mung beans! Yum!

Blog entry 21st March
Fitness levels and recovery time.
I've never been one to 'work out' or go 'jogging'.
Hubby and I enjoy going out for lovely long walks together, keeping up a reasonable pace and we get to spend that quality time together whilst exercising.
Hubby works as a Builder and I enjoy going out to work with him, getting physical with the wheel barrow and heavy lifting is fun.

One thing I have noticed is that before I went raw/alkaline when we had work that involved the really heavy stuff it would take most of the week for my aching muscles to recover.

Now I'm mostly raw and in particular pH neutral (which I believe is very significant btw).

This last 2 weeks we have spent cutting down and shredding some very large conifers, followed by lots of digging (Hubby) and barrowing (Me), which was followed by more shovelling and barrowing (both of us).

I noticed that my muscles only had moderate ache which disappeared by the next day. Nothing like the 'shredded muscles hanging off' kind of feeling that I had last year for 3 weeks when we dug out and barrowed a whole stone wall into a skip.

Also I have noticed I have much more muscle definition than my previous efforts.

And most of all I FEEL SOOO GOOD!!! Right through!

Raw is definitely good for the body and speeds up recovery time, but I do believe that bringing my saliva levels up from pH 5.0 to pH 7.0 has been a major contributor in the healing process.

Blog entry 14th may 2010
The D is back.... for a while!
From time to time I can't seem to control myself and eat copious amounts of what I term a 'standard western diet'.
To add insult to injury Hubby and I just returned from spending a week in Ontario, Canada where we did more of

the same. (The trip was great btw)
Now we have returned, my whole body is rebelling against this constant barrage of acidic foods.
My breathing is changed (a sure indicator of my general condition overall) and I get out of breath quite easily.
I also developed a nice throat infection on our return. My body really is showing me how unhappy and full of toxins it is.
The throat is yucky, and my blood sugars are well into diabetes numbers again. Fasting blood sugars this morning 7.4 mmols!!! Yep a good ol' infection for sure!

I've made real efforts to eat more alkaline since I returned home, both raw and cooked. Drinking lots of lemon and honey drinks to help my throat and raise my alkaline levels (the honey isn't actually alkaline but does help to temper the lemon flavour) the key here really is to consume as much alkaline as I can to support my body in its repair phase.

Sodium bicarbonate seems to help to soothe the soreness of the throat too, as well as adding to the alkalising effect.
I feel better in myself today although my throat is very sore to talk.

Saliva levels are back up to pH 6.25 today so I know my efforts are paying off.

Blog entry 18th may 2010
Slow recovery, but getting there.
The throat infection I have been experiencing since my return from vacation in Canada is still bothersome but less so than the last few days thank goodness.
My blood sugars have been coming back down into normal ranges during the day now although those fasting blood sugars are still 7.1mmols each day. A combination of better quality alkaline meals, the ability to increase my activity levels along with the passing in general of the virus itself all seem to be contributing to my better blood sugars and a very much improved pH levels today too.

Blog entry 24th may 2010
Set back.
This ghastly virus is still causing me issues! Whilst my throat is very much improved I now have the added discomfort of almost uncontrollable diarrhoea! I have no idea how I came to get it, I feel tired but otherwise quite well.
Fasting blood sugars are still raised, 6.7mmols this morning. I still wonder if this is down to the amount of stress I put on my body whilst away on vacation. I mean donuts, dairy, bread, you name it I was eating it!
So is this my body's way of having a really good detox?? Perhaps.

Blog entry 25th may 2010
Much better now!
Finally! I feel much better today for the first time in 2 weeks.
I had two very small meals yesterday, really the nausea was so bad all I could tolerate was ginger tea.
Well it seemed to have worked.
I didn't eat anything after 2pm yesterday afternoon.
Blood sugars at bedtime were 4.8mmols.
Fasting blood sugars were 6.7mmols
something is still lurking somewhere in the background.
I ate half my breakfast this morning, at least my appetite is coming back on line.... if only half of it.
I can feel some gardening coming on........

JB thought that I may have picked up some kind of parasitic critter (Giardia) whilst on my travels. I took a couple of drops of food grade Hydrogen Peroxide in water for a couple of weeks which seemed to help to eradicate the beasties. They are notoriously difficult to get rid of!
Anyway no signs of any more parasites in the system now so fingers crossed I managed to get rid of them successfully.

Blog entry 27th may 2010
Normal Again.
With great relief I can now report that 2 mornings on the trot my fasting blood sugars has been in normal ranges.
HURRAY!
Yesterday was 5.1mmols then 5.5mmols this morning.

Sticking to more of the alkaline foods list now too, even picked some young nettles in the garden and made a bean and nettle stew with them, it was pretty darn good!

Blog entry 5th June 2010
What's to eat?
Following the success of my conversion to a mostly raw alkalizing diet to really control diabetes I do get asked quite a bit about what can be eaten or not eaten when adopting this lifestyle change.
You are right in thinking that the lists giving the Alkalising foods can vary a little. Some basic 'rules' seem to apply though which are relatively easy to implement when you are high raw anyway.
Green veggies win hands down, as do sprouted legumes and seeds,
Many fruits are alkalising, some are acidic. Surprisingly lemons and tomatoes despite being acidic fruits are actually highly alkalising, so I'm afraid testing the food directly would be useless here.
Most nuts are a no-no except almonds which are very alkalising. Peanuts are the worst.
Good oils include extra virgin olive, hemp, coconut, flax, avocado.... you get the picture
Ancient grains may be mildly alkalising or even neutral, they are very alkalising once sprouted.
Potatoes may only be eaten when they have skins on, baby new potatoes, baked jacket potatoe and sweet potatoe are also very alkalising.
Off the list are meat, eggs, fish, dairy, alcohol, tobacco, processed foods, deep fried foods, modern grains, pickles and condiments, and sugar.

So the basic rule is to keep it fresh, and eat it in its most natural state as much as possible.
An alkalising diet usually is made up of at least 70% alkalising foods, the rest can be made up of some of the acidic foods if you wish.

I test my saliva first thing in the morning, holding the pH test strip against the cheek of my mouth (by the salivary glands), some foods that show up rather ambiguous on differing lists may or may not change my pH levels.
Apple cider vinegar for instance is raved about as being alkalising, but it definitely has an acidic effect on me.
Balsamic vinegar is alkalising for me.

The main question I get from the diabetic forums is 'My carbs need to be limited in order to manage blood glucose levels, what can I snack on?' Well you can still snack on seeds, nuts, and raw non-starchy veggies.

Once the alkalising starts to affect your body you find you can eat more freely, many people feel more energised, they feel 'clean.' My own friends comment on how good my complexion is and how sparkly my eyes are.

I do feel different when I am eating high alkaline, more spark, with a spring in my step, I just ooze 'feel good factor', and apparently I 'glow'. Cool!

Blog entry date 6th July 2010
Still doing well.

Tomorrow heralds another visit to the Diabetologist for my second visit this year. This is my 4th D-versary.

My previous visit was in January, they are puzzled by my apparent success with the Alkaline diet although won't admit it saying that aggressive Insulin treatment and a change in diet and losing lots of weight was what prompted my recovery.

Fact is that weight loss was only a few pounds, certainly not enough to prompt my reduction from 24 units of insulin each day down to zero...in 5 weeks!

I had been on Insulin therapy for 3 years, they even told me I was Latent Type 1.

And I most certainly don't eat a zero carb diet. I eat well. I eat fresh and Alkaline as much as possible. I do keep a count of my carb intake for any given meal, though I can get sleepy after a hearty meal.

Fasting blood sugars this morning were 5.4mmols.

Recent test results were:

HbA1c 5.3

Cholesterol 3.8

Kidneys, liver etc all functioning normally.

I still take the pancreatic supplements Alpha Lipoic Acid, Vitamin D3, and Chromium Picolinate.

So overall I am still doing well, and very pleased with myself.

Hopefully the specialist won't want to see me for another 12 months.

Blog entry date 15th July 2010
D clinic visit...... report.
I am still amazed and rather pleased with my visit to see the Diabetologist last week.

First of all he asked me how I am getting along, and when I announced that' I am VERY well thank you' he then asked me if I was still eating 'that cabbage diet'.
Well yes I am still eating a mostly alkalising diet (as much as possible).

He poo-poo'ed the whole alkalising thing (which I was expecting) but he was more than happy with my recent blood results.

We mutually decided that I no longer need to visit him at the clinic and I can now continue to just deal with my family practitioner, he did point out that I can go back to the clinic if the need arises.

I think that is a really great result, and I am very pleased with myself....now where is the 'pat yourself on the back' emoticon....??

This is a great result and I can now continue the good work with the alkaline foods.
Conventional medicine may not agree about this diet but it most assuredly works for me!

Alkalise your life!

Liquidizing your meals will aid the body to process food into usable energy quickly. This is a very important step in your healing process.
These recipes should help to get you started.

Basic Smoothie recipe
250ml filtered water/ almond nut mylk/soya milk (whatever suits)
A third of a cucumber
Juice of half a lemon
Add other soft ingredients and blend (except avocado)
Then add tougher ingredients and blend until desired consistency.
Add avocado here if you are including it, it makes the whole thing very thick and gloopy.
Add sea salt to taste.
Add other flavourings.
I got on better eating from a bowl with a spoon (a green 'soup') as some of these recipes are impossible from a glass!
Don't forget to chew your smoothies! It helps the digestion process.
To make my 'soups' more fun I add sprinkles of linseeds, coconut or sunflower seeds etc for added crunch.

Other variations:
Kale and pear.
Kale, cucumber and ginger.
Kale, apple and ginger.
Spinach, cucumber and watercress.
Broccoli, cucumber and sunflower seed sprouts.
Smoothies can be really versatile, and you can use what you have in the fridge.

The following list will help you to more easily bring your body's pH levels back into line.

In the morning drink a glass of water with the juice of half a lemon. Although lemon is acid by nature it has an amazing alkalising effect on the body. You can drink this as often as you like.

Make lentils, sweet potatoes, yams, and other root crops your staples. These foods help to alkalise the body quickly.

Eat green vegetables at least once per day. They are full of important vitamins, minerals, and beneficial phyto compounds as well as being very alkalising.

Add Miso, seaweeds, ginger, and daikon radish to your dishes. As well as being alkalising they aid digestion and add some spice to your dishes.

Eat non-glutinous grains. Choose Quinoa, Amaranth, Wild rice, Brown rice and also Buckwheat. These will provide important Amino Acids to your diet.

Substitute Alkalizing root crops instead of pasta, potatoes and breads and grains products. Choose yams, sweet potatoes, rutabaga, jicama, burdock, lotus root, taro root, onion, kohlrabi, parsnips, and beets.

Eat several servings of fresh fruit daily, especially as snacks. Fruit salads are a great way to include a variety of nutrient rich alkalizing foods in your diet.

Drink spring or filtered water, especially high in a mineral content.

Consume fresh green vegetable juices as they are great Alkalisers.

Consider adding an Alkalizing supplement to your diet for additional support. A Super Greens powder is suggested here.

Each night at bedtime take half a teaspoon of bicarbonate of soda in a glass of water, swish around your mouth before swallowing. This must be at least 3 hours after food so as not to affect the natural digestive process of your stomach.

Vegetables
Spinach.
Kale.
Broccoli.
Asparagus.
Artichoke (Jerusalem).
Aubergine.
Beetroots (limited amounts).
Bean sprouts.
Broccoli.
Brussels sprouts.
Burdock root.
Cabbage (red, white, Chinese).
Carrots (limited amounts).

Cauliflower.
Celery.
Cucumber.
Garlic.
Green and yellow Squash.
Green beans.
Greens of any kind.
Kale.
Kelp.
Kohlrabi.
Leek.
Lettuce.
Okra.
Onions.
Parsley.
Parsnips.
Fresh peas.
Radishes.
Bell peppers. Red, yellow and green.
Salsify.
Sea vegetables, Wakame, Nori, Hijiki.
Spinach.
Spring onions.
Sprouted grains beans of seeds.
Swedes.
Turnips.
Water chestnuts.
Winter squash (limited amounts).
Grasses, Wheat grass, Barley grass, Oat grass, etc.
Watercress.

High carbohydrate vegetables (may be included in the 20% of your diet).
Sweet potatoes.
Beetroot.
Carrots.
Baby new potatoes.
Red skinned potatoes (with skins)(these are usually fresher).
Winter squash (acorn, butternut, pumpkin).
Yams.
Parsnip.

Fruits
Avocado.
Apple (baked or raw).
Apricots.

Bananas.
Blackberries.
Blueberries.
Cantaloupe melon (eat it alone or leave it alone! This ferments in the gut when eaten with other foods!).
Currants.
Dates.
Kiwi.
Oranges, tangerines, mandarins.
Mango.
Papaya.
Peach.
Pear.
Pineapple.
Raisins.
Raspberries.
Strawberries.
Tomatoe.
Lemon.
Lime.
Grapefruit (check if this interacts with any of your prescribed medicines!).
Unripe banana.
Sour cherry.
Fresh coconut.
Watermelon(eat it alone or leave it alone! This ferments in the gut when eaten with other foods!).
Honeydew melon (eat it alone or leave it alone! This ferments in the gut when eaten with other foods!).

Grains (may be included in the 20% of your diet) these are neutral or slightly acidic.
Spelt.
Buckwheat.
Quinoa.
Millet.
Amaranth.
Legumes.
Soy beans (frozen, tofu, dried soy nuts).
Lentils.
Fresh peas.

Nuts/Seeds
Almond (very alkalizing) try soaking them for 4 hours before eating them, it's easier on the digestion.
Brazil.
Cashews.

Coconut.
Hazel.
Pumpkin.
Sesame.
Sunflower.
Linseeds.
Chestnuts.
Macadamia.

Sprouts
Mung bean sprouts.
Adzuki beans.
Sprouted lentils.
Sunflower seeds.
Buckwheat.
Any seed/grain that may be sprouted.
Wheat grass.
Oat grass.
Barley grass.

Herbs and Spices
Fresh is best but dried are okay, herbs and spices will add flavour to many of your dishes.
Pink Himalayan salt (marvellous!!!).
Sea salt (pure, no anti caking agents).
Ginger.
Garlic.
Miso.
Apple cider vinegar in moderation.
Horseradish.

Oils ~ cold pressed virgin oils
Olive.
Coconut.
Linseed.
Flaxseed.
Avocado.
Sesame seed.
Evening primrose.

Dairy alternatives
Soy milk.
Almond mylk.
Water, filtered or mineral.

FOODS TO AVOID
Red meat.
Corn.
Glutinous grains (wheat, rye, barley, processed oats).
Artificial sweeteners (Stevia is a natural plant extract from S. America which is very sweet and an excellent alternative to sugar and sweeteners).
Sugar.
Fish.
Shellfish.
Peanuts (very high in fungus/moulds!).
Alcohol.
Coffee.
Black tea (some non-caffeine herbals ore okay but not fruity ones).
Fruit juices from concentrate or processed juices (fresh squeezed is best).
Nicotine products (cigars, cigarettes).
Soda drinks.
Yeast.
Dairy (milk, cheese, yoghurt).
Fungus (mushrooms, Quorn).
Fermented products (mayonnaise, ketchup, vinegar, pickles, soy sauce [try Braggs Liquid Aminos instead of soy sauce])

How to prepare your foods
Raw (sliced, diced, grated, whole)
Steamed (don't overdo it, just lightly steamed is far better than being overcooked. Steaming means that you can eat warmer meals occasionally whilst adjusting to your new lifestyle)
Juices.
Smoothies.
Fried? Try not to. It only acidifies your foods.
Baked. Great for potatoes and squashes.

Be sure that your meals are made up of at least 80% alkalizing foods and a maximum of 20% acidic/neutral foods.
The more you can stick to the Alkalizing diet the better your chances of changing your pH levels will be.
Falling off the wagon may happen occasionally, don't worry just make sure your next meals are super Alkalizing to balance it out.

Recipe section.

In this section I have included some of my favourite Alkalising recipes, you may like to include some of your favourite ingredients or change the ingredients to suit what is available seasonally for you at the time.
Whichever way you do it, enjoy your meals.

Almond Nut Mylk
Ingredients.
2 cups almonds
6 cups purified water
2-3 medjool dates

Directions.
Soak almonds for 4 hours or more
Place almonds and water in a blender on high speed.
Strain mixture through a nut milk bag or a couple layers of cheese cloth in to a bowl.
Rinse blender and add back in the strained liquid.
Add dates and blend.
Mix with any of your favourite soft fruits to make delicious fruit smoothies.

Smoothie.
Ingredients.
1 Avocado
Around 400mls Almond nut 'milk'/soya milk (unsweetened)
a tablespoon of coconut flakes
squeeze of Lemon juice

Directions.
Blend all ingredients in liquidizer.
Serve immediately.

Breakfast Smoothie.
Ingredients.
½ large grapefruit (remove skin, pith & seeds)
A handful of sprouted seeds (alfalfa, clover or others)
A handful of fresh spinach leaves
1/3 cup fresh ground flaxseeds
1-2 tbsp olive oil
2 cups chopped broccoli (raw)
½ cup chopped cucumber
1 and ½ cups purified water

Directions.
Place water, oil, cucumber and spinach leaves in liquidizer.
Blend on medium speed, or high speed for smoother blend.
Add Broccoli, ground flaxseeds and grapefruit.
Blend until desired consistency.
Serve and enjoy!

Tip.
I enjoyed half of what I made, then I was full up so kept the rest in the fridge until lunchtime

Coconut, Spinach & Kale Smoothie.

This morning's 'smoothie' has been made from a few simple ingredients which all get blitzed in the blender.

1 avocado
handful of kale
handful of spinach
250 ml soya milk (organic/unsweetened)
tablespoon of dried coconut
handful of dried almonds
juice of half a lemon
pinch sea salt
tablespoon olive oil
half teaspoon dried ginger

sounds gross doesn't it?? yet it's so creamy and almost like porridge, and despite the light green colour.
It's absolutely delicious. I make variations of this every morning, and as it makes enough for 2 servings I will finish it off with some crunchy veggies dipped in it for lunch Yum!!!

Green Smoothie.

handful of raw broccoli or kale
handful of raw spinach
250ml soya milk
juice 1 lemon
third of a cucumber
half a cup of sprouted sunflower seeds
2 tablespoon olive oil
sea salt
1 avocado

I eat half of this for breakfast

Colossal Fruit Salad Breakfast.

Ingredients.
1 small banana
1 small apple
1 kiwi
a tablespoon of mango
1 tablespoon of pineapple
a chunk of ginger chopped
some olive oil
half juice lemon
sunflower seeds
raw cacao nibs
and sea salt.

Method
Peel and slice all fruit into bite sized pieces.
Mix remaining ingredients and pour over fruit.
Eat and enjoy!

Vegan Scrambled Eggs.

½ pack firm Tofu
Sprinkle of ground turmeric
Sprinkle of ground ginger
Tbsp olive oil
Small red onion, chopped
A handful of chopped kale
Avocado
Cucumber
Tomato
Sea salt

Method.
Drain Tofu, and pat dry with kitchen paper.
Crumble tofu, sprinkle with turmeric, ginger and salt.
Gently stir fry with chopped onions and kale until hot all through. (Around 3-4 minutes).
Serve with fresh avocado, tomatoes and cucumber.

Packed Lunch.

This is what my husband terms my 'nosebag' of raw veggies which I can munch on all day when we are away from home or at work.

Zucchini/courgette
Bell pepper (red, yellow or green)
Cucumber
Tomatoes
Celery
Sliced sweet potato
Radish
Cauliflower
Broccoli
Green beans
Carrots
Apples
Bananas
Apricots
Pineapple

Use lettuce leaves or nori sheets and have a 'wrap' of your favourite veggies.

And why not make yourself a green smoothie or juice and put it into a flask.

You can have goodness on the run.

Courgette and Turmeric Soup

Ingredients
4 large courgettes chopped
1 large or 2 small onions chopped
2 bay leaves
1 heaped teaspoon turmeric
sea salt
pepper
boiled water
olive oil

Method
sauté chopped courgettes and onions in olive oil until soft
add turmeric, bay leaves
add enough water to cover the veg
season with salt and pepper to taste (i find this recipe takes quite a bit of salt)
simmer until soft
remove bay leaves
liquidize until smooth
serve with crusty garlic bread

NB don't try adding garlic to the recipe as it ruins the delicate flavour!

It freezes really well too.

Asparagus with Lime and Mint.

Ingredients.
1 lb. of asparagus, trimmed
1 ½ tablespoons of olive oil
Sea salt
Fresh ground pepper
1-2 fresh limes
1 teaspoon of fresh mint,

Method.
1 Heat the oil in a wide sauté or frying pan on medium-high. When the oil is hot, add the asparagus and sprinkle with salt and pepper to taste, cooking for about 5 minutes until fragrant.
2 Put on a plate and squeeze lime juice over the asparagus and sprinkle on the mint.

Roasted Cauliflower.

Ingredients.
1 head of cauliflower
2-3 cloves of garlic, peeled and coarsely minced
Lemon juice from half a lemon
Olive oil
Coarse salt and freshly ground black pepper

Method.
Preheat oven to 180°C.
Cut cauliflower into florets and put in a single layer in an oven-proof baking dish. Toss in the garlic. Sprinkle lemon juice over cauliflower and drizzle each piece with olive oil. Sprinkle with salt and pepper.
Place casserole in the hot oven, uncovered, for 25-30 minutes, or until the top is lightly brown. Test with a fork for desired doneness. Fork should be able to easily pierce the cauliflower.
Remove from oven and serve immediately.

Roasted Mediterrean Vegetables

Ingredients
1 medium Aubergine/Eggplant
1 medium Courgette/Zucchini
1 bell pepper
1 head of garlic, (leave in skins, separate cloves)
Handful of Baby tomatoes
olive oil
ground coriander, cumin, and smoked paprika
juice of one lemon
salt and pepper to taste

Method
Preheat the oven to 200 degrees.
Cut veggies into similar sized pieces.
Put the eggplant and zucchini pieces into a roasting pan or baking dish.
Sprinkle fairly liberally with salt and drizzle with olive oil.
Dust with coriander, cumin, and paprika, tossing to coat.
Roast in the oven for about 30 minutes, stir a couple of times, until the vegetables are tender and just a little bit browned on the edges.
Put the vegetables into a bowl, toss with lemon juice and additional olive oil to taste, and season with salt and pepper.

Grilled Fish with Wild and Brown Rice.

Rice.
½ cup brown rice
½ cup of wild rice
2 cups cold water
Sea salt
Bring to boil and simmer for 30 minutes or until all water is absorbed.

Fish
Filet of fish (Haddock, Trout, Cod, or similar)
Slice of fresh lemon
Drizzle of olive oil.
Wrap fish, lemon, olive oil in foil and bake on 200C for 18-20 mins depending on size of fish.

Vinaigrette.
¼ cup extra virgin olive oil
2 tablespoon fresh lemon juice
¾ tsp minced fresh garlic
¾ tsp sea salt
Freshly cracked black pepper
Pinch dried thyme
Mix gently and serve drizzled over fish and rice.

Avocado and Crunchy Veggie Salad.

Ingredients.
1 Beef tomato sliced
½ red Bell pepper sliced
½ yellow Bell pepper sliced
1 cup of small broccoli florets
1 cup small cauliflower florets
Mixed green salad leaves (spinach, watercress and rocket)

Dressing
Juice of 1 lemon
¼ cup of Olive oil
¾ teaspoon Sea salt
Chilli pepper
Mixed herbs.

Directions.
Arrange salad leaves and beef tomato on plate.
Mix dressing.
Place bell peppers, broccoli and cauli in a salad bowl and pour dressing over mixing well to coat all veggies.
Serve on top of the bed of leaves & tomatoes.

Quinoa Tabbouleh.

This version of Tabbouleh made with Quinoa, I had about a serving spoon portion with some broccoli and cauliflower and a nice piece of baked salmon.

Ingredients.
1 cup uncooked quinoa
2 cups Water
1 large bunch parsley chopped
1 small bunch mint chopped
5 small tomatoes, diced
1 onion, finely diced
1 lemon, juiced
Salt to taste.

Directions.
Rinse quinoa in a sieve.
Place in a saucepan with 2 cups of cold water and cover. Bring to the boil and simmer for 20 minutes or until soft and the water has been absorbed. (quinoa is cooked when its 'tails' are showing).
Mix all other ingredients with Quinoa and serve.

Raw Spicy Pesto Sauce.

Ingredients.
half a cup of sunflower seeds
juice of 1 lemon
olive oil
half fresh chilli pepper(including the seeds)
Braggs aminos to taste (a soy sauce)
teaspoon fresh ginger (or to taste)
tablespoon of desiccated coconut

Method.
Blitzed in the blender until smooth, or less time if you prefer it chunky.

Serve with dinner over courgettes (thinly sliced longways, like raw vegetable noodles) or use it as a dip for crunchy chopped veggies.

Spicy Vegetable salad with Sweet Potato.

Ingredients
Sweet potato (raw, peeled and grated)
1 cup Broccoli florets
1 cup cauliflower florets
1 cup Cherry tomatoes
1 cup of sliced cucumber
1 stick of celery, sliced
Spinach, raw

Dressing
$\frac{1}{4}$ cup Olive oil
Juice of 1 lemon
1 clove Garlic crushed
Fresh chilli chopped (remove seeds unless you like it really hot!)
1tsp Coriander, $\frac{1}{2}$ tsp Cumin, $\frac{1}{4}$ tsp Ginger,
Salt and pepper to taste

Method.
Arrange bed of spinach on plate.
Chop veggies.
Arrange on plate on top of bed of spinach.
Mix dressing well and
drizzle dressing all over veggies.

Absolutely delicious!

Chunky Raw Vegetable Salad.

Ingredients.
raw broccoli florets
raw cauliflower florets
raw spinach/rocket leaves
raw baby tomatoes
raw sweet potatoe sliced
sunflower seeds
raw whole hemp seeds
sesame seeds
cracked pink Himalayan salt
juice half fresh lemon
olive oil
sprinkle some herbs

Method.
Arrange all ingredients on plate
Make vinaigrette and pour over veggies.
Eat and enjoy.

that is the same formula for most of my meals, but I then I add one of the following

2 boiled/scrambled eggs
tablespoon quinoa/amaranth/brown rice
tablespoon of hummus
sliced avocado

Hubbies Famous Chunky Tomato Sauce.

Ingredients.
2 medium Courgette
2 Bell peppers
2 medium Red onion
200g Chestnut mushrooms
2 cans Tinned tomatoes
3 cloves Garlic finely chopped
$\frac{1}{4}$ tsp Fenugreek
White wine
Balsamic vinegar
Salt
Black pepper
Basil

Method
Chop all veggies to similar size, keeping them fairly chunky.
Gently fry onions and garlic until soft.
Add all chunky veggies and fry until soft.
Add fenugreek.
Add white wine, and all other seasoning.
Simmer until all veggies are cooked through and sauce is reduced a bit.
Best made the day before you eat it to allow flavours to infuse.

Broccoli and Tofu Stir fry.

Ingredients.
1 bunch broccoli, chopped
1 onion, chopped
4 cloves garlic, crushed
2 carrots, sliced
1 lb. drained tofu, sliced into chunks
Braggs amino's
$\frac{1}{4}$ tsp ground ginger
Dried chilli powder
Sesame oil
Lime juice.

Method.
Slice all veggies thinly.
Coat drained dried tofu with dried ginger, chilli and Braggs Amino's.
Heat wok or skillet on medium/hot heat.
Add small amount of sesame oil until very hot. Add all ingredients except lime juice and cook until tender.
Drizzle lime juice over the top.
Serve and eat immediately.

Green Soya Bean Stir Fry.

Ingredients.
½ a Yellow pepper (sliced)
½ a red pepper (sliced)
200g of frozen Soya Beans
2 sticks of celery (cut diagonally)
1 small (200g) packet of bean sprouts
65g of spring onions (cut diagonally)
1 garlic clove (finely chopped)
½ inch grated ginger
1tbsp of olive oil
Dash of Braggs Amino's
Juice from ½ lime.

Method.
Heat the oil in a wok, add the garlic, celery and spring onions and fry for about 1 min
Add the peppers, mushrooms and Soya Beans, fry for a couple of minutes
Add the bean sprouts and sauce and cook for two further minutes
Finish off with the lime juice.

Cauliflower Tabbouleh.

Ingredients.
a third of a medium sized fresh cauliflower
one red onion ~ diced
1 medium tomatoe~ diced
a third of cucumber ~ diced
one yellow bell pepper ~ diced
sea salt or few drops of braggs aminos to taste
black pepper (optional)
half fresh chilli pepper chopped very small with seeds if you dare ! (optional)
juice of one lemon
1 clove garlic crushed.
third of a cup of olive oil
fresh parsley
handful of pumpkin seeds

Method.
Grate the cauliflower to look like couscous.
Dice rest of veggies.
Mix everything in a big bowl and serve on a bed of green leaves and enjoy!

Spicy Raw Tomato Sauce.

Last night I had some buckwheat for dinner with the usual veggies and a nice 'raw' sauce poured over it. It was really quite tasty...

Ingredients.
3 tomatoes
half fresh red chilli, use the seeds as well if you're brave!
1 avocado
a dash of Braggs amino (or soy sauce)
tablespoon of olive oil
juice of 1 lemon
tablespoon of sunflower seeds

Method.
Blitz it all in the blender until smooth then serve.

Vinaigrette dressing.

Making a Vinaigrette dressing using lemon juice. Olive oil and your favourites herbs and spices and drizzle over any of your meals. This is a super Alkalising addition to any of your meals.

Ingredients
Juice of 1 lemon
¼ cup of Olive oil
¾ teaspoon Sea salt
Cayenne pepper
Mixed herbs.

Method.
Gently mix ingredients and serve.

Alternatives.
Make it hot and spicy with Indian spices if you prefer a kick.

Add 1 tablespoon white miso for a thick creamy sauce similar to mayonnaise.

Try adding Chopped fresh herbs like Basil, Thyme, Oregano or Tarragon.

Frozen Fruit Pudding

Ingredients.
handful of frozen strawberries
one medium banana
some almond flour
a little soya milk or nut mylk.

Method.
Take a cup of fresh strawberries, sliced and frozen.
Take a cup of fresh banana, sliced and frozen.
whizz fruit in the food processor until smooth,
add almond flour and a little soya milk to make creamy consistency.
....and enjoy soft homemade ice-cream!

Best served and eaten immediately.

Also enjoyable with Blueberries instead of Strawberries.

The Complete Blood Sugar Results Table

Date	Time	Value	TBR
2nd July	21.25	5.0mmols	
3rd July	06.53	4.7	
3rd July	11.45	4.3	
3rd July	15.23	4.6	
3rd July	17.15	4.5	
3rd July	19.20	5.6	
3rd July	21.55	4.1	90% TBR
4th July	06.15	4.4	
4th July	09.25	4.7	
4th July	11.19	4.4	
4th July	12.50	4.6	
4th July	14.30	5.9	
4th July	15.32	6.5	
4th July	16.43	5.3	
4th July	18.33	5.4	
4th July	20.53	4.6	
5Th July	03.30	4.4	80%TBR
5th July	06.55	4.7	
5th July	08.47	4.9	
5th July	10.10	5.2	
5th July	12.00	4.7	70% TBR
5th July	13.40	6.2	
5th July	15.19	4.7	
5th July	17.09	4.9	

Date	Time	Value	Note
5th July	21.13	5.7	
6th July	02.41	4.1	
6th July	05.00	4.6	
6th July	08.19	8.0	30g carbs
6th July	10.03	6.2	
6th July	12.01	5.4	
6th July	13.33	8.5	20g carbs
6th July	15.19	5.8	
6th July	16.46	5.7	
6th July	18.32	4.6	
6th July	19.46	4.9	
6th July	22.46	4.7	
7th July	01.22	4.2	
7th July	06.56	4.3	
7th July	12.02	4.8	
7th July	16.05	4.1	
7th July	22.19	4.0	
8th July	01.59	3.8	
8th July	05.08	3.3	
8th July	05.37	4.5	carrot juice
8th July	06.39	5.4	
8th July	10.30	4.1	
8th July	12.01	6.8	
8th July	13.23	3.9	
8th July	16.23	5.3	60%TBR
8th July	21.22	4.9	
8th July	23.00	4.6	
9th July	04.00	3.9	
9th July	06.54	3.7	Carrot juice
9th July	12.00	4.2	Carrot juice
9th July	16.10	3.8	50%TBR carrot juice
9th July	16.51	6.0	
9th July	22.20	4.6	
10th July	02.40	3.7	carrot juice
10th July	06.32	3.9	40%TBR
10th July	12.13	4.9	
10th July	14.50	4.8	
10th July	16.00	4.9	
10th July	21.03	4.9	
11th July	02.25	4.1	
11th July	07.51	4.1	
11th July	11.21	4.2	
11th July	16.53	4.7	
11th July	18.45	5.9	
11th July	19.53	5.5	

Date	Time	Value	Notes
11th July	22.00	5.0	
12th July	00.05	4.9	
12th July	05.23	4.3	
12th July	08.11	5.6	30%TBR
12th July	11.00	5.2	
12th July	13.00	5.0	
12th July	21.31	4.8	
13th July	06.33	4.1	
13th July	08.30	4.6	
13th July	11.33	4.8	
13th July	13.01	5.2	
13th July	19.07	5.3	
13th July	22.01	4.8	
14th July	06.31	5.2	
14th July	08.11	5.7	
14th July	09.53	5.7	
19th July		4.3	fasting blood
19th July		6.5	before golf
19th July		5.5	after 2 hrs golf
20th July			20% Basal
21st July		5.0	fasting blood
22nd July	18.25	8.2	
22nd July	21.15	6.1	
23rd July	02.45	5.3	
23rd July	07.45	5.6	
23rd July	20.30	5.6	
23rd July	22.25	6.0	
23rd July	23.55	6.2	
24th July	07.10	5.9	
24th July	11.55	5.7	
24th July	14.15	4.8	
24th July	19.00	7.5	
24th July	21.55	5.2	
25th July	05.35	5.6	
25th July	08.10	7.2	
25th July	10.10	5.4	
25th July	12.40	6.4	
25th July	15.10	5.0	
25th July	18.30	6.7	50g carbs
25th July	20.00	8.9	
25th July	21.40	8.5	
25th July	22.20	7.9	
26th July	05.45	6.3	
26th July	08.32	6.0	
3rd August			total removal of Insulin Pump
23rd August			Final correction dose of Insulin.

CPSIA information can be obtained
at www.ICGtesting.com
Printed in the USA
LVHW110955170619
621456LV00001B/8/P